GRIMOIRE SYMPATHIA
— THE WORKSHOP
OF THE INFINITE

I-H-O BOOKS

GRIMOIRE
SYMPATHIA

THE WORKSHOP
OF THE INFINITE:

HEALING WITHOUT MEDICINE USING

THE SPIRITUAL ESSENCE OF PLANTS,

MINERALS AND PRECIOUS STONES.

BY

CHARUBEL

EDITED BY A. R. NAYLOR

ISBN 1-872189-49-0

I-H-O Books © 2003
Essex House, Thame, England. OX9 3LS.

Originally published as
*Psychology of Botany, Minerals
and Precious Stones*.
Robert Welch.
Tyldesley. 1906

EDITOR'S NOTE

Charubel (1826–1906) is best known today for his book *The Degrees of the Zodiac Symbolised*. The present work was originally published by Robert Welch in 1906 as the *Psychology of Botany, Minerals and Precious Stones* (being a revised edition of what had appeared serially in the *Psychic Mirror*). It appears that the work may have been published posthumously — the dedication to Robert Welch contains the bequest "to whom I leave all my works and manuscripts for publication, and use as articles for magazines, &c., &c., " — on the last page of the book Mr R. Welch is also attributed as Editor.

The published text contains many inconsistencies in the presentation of the data, together with numerous typographical errors and spelling mistakes. This somewhat careless editorial and book production by Robert Welch contrasts quite sharply with the author's scholarship and extensive vocabulary.

The 1906 edition also includes a number of disparate botanical illustrations of varying quality taken from divers sources — evidence suggests that these pictures may have been included by Robert Welch and not Charubel. It was decided to exclude these illustrations not only for their inappropriateness but moreover because it appears that

Welch (if he was indeed responsible for their selection) was not sufficiently familiar with the text of the book — Charubel writes :–

> " There are, however, cheap books in the market, devoted to Descriptive Botany, I consider it needless, I should waste time, and occupy space, on such a line when the same might be purchased at a bookstall. I shall confine myself to what cannot be purchased otherwise than by reading my revelations.

From this it is quite clear that Charubel would not waste twenty-two pages on such pictures, but the reader should not assume that it is unnecessary to have any botanical knowledge, as Charubel extolls the study of the natural world as a necessary prerequisite for any self-respecting magician or occultist. He states :–

> Some pride themselves in their supposed attainments in occult knowledge; just test that wisdom beside these researches which I am publishing under the *Psychology of Botany*. If your instincts, fail to conduct you into the spirit which pervades these Revelations. If you fail to appreciate these truths, cease hereafter to consider yourselves Occultists, much less Magicians. Remember this: to become a Magician you must become a student of nature at first hand.

Furthermore, on the subject of Occultists he later states :–

There is a sham Occultism, and there is a genuine one; the former gives lectures and reconnoitres every city, town, village and hamlet, in his search for proselytes. He seeks publicity in all those fashionable and popular devices now current, and like his prototype, the Pharisee of old, he does all to be seen of men. As a next subterfuge, he slanders the individual, and stigmatises such Divine Inspirations given forth by him with the opprobrious epithet "Obsession." Thus proving descent from those who told the Christ of history to his face that he had a devil. If they, the fathers of modern hypocrites, called the "Master of the house Beelzebub, how much more they of his household."

The genuine Occultist seeks not publicity in order to promote his own popularity, or that of his philosophy. He may be desirous that all should become acquainted with the leading principles of his system of Philosophy, considering such a move a step in the right direction. The true Occultist, conscious of the wealth he possesses in that wisdom, the price of which exceeds that of rubies; he unavoidably feels a species of independency which the riches of this world cannot afford. He feels strong in the truth of his Lord, and in the power of his might, in that he has found the way to that hidden manna. He has opened a fountain in the flinty rock, the water follows him, he has drank of it, it is henceforth within him a well of water, springing up into life eternal.

Charubel was born a seer and clairvoyant and he used his psychic abilities to ascertain the nature and influence of each degree for his book *The Degrees of the Zodiac Symbolised*. Charubel accomplished his astrological task unaided, producing an original work not copied from any other author, ancient or modern. Over the years many have studied Charubel's symbols and are convinced that by whatever means they were obtained, whether *supernormal* or not, they have a definite and a substantial basis.

The present work was also obtained psychically but it has lain fallow for almost one hundred years. Charubel's ideas were far ahead of his time and show great insight. His concept of empathic healing, using the positive and negative energy of the soul plane, combined with his use of sigils, colour aura and invocations, is unique. At times he expresses strong views as he expounds his precepts :–

When an Occultist speaks of the Feminine, or the Masculine, it must be borne in mind that such terms are not used by him as distinguishing marks of gender. I know such terms are bandied about very freely by a number of writers in such a light as to beget very absurd notions respecting this subject, simply because the mind of the writer has failed to grasp the true idea as to what is implied by the terms Masculine and Feminine.

Men go to write on these sublime themes steeped in the filth of their own animality; and with dirty fingers pollute those pages of wisdom found in nature, that book of God, stereotyped in ineffaceable characters on the fiery ether, that ever unfolding Scrowl. But he who has wisdom will detect the sham from the genuine coin. . . .

. . . I make known to you one of the grand mysteries of heaven: It is with the Negative side of Divinity that we have to do. It is the Mother side of Deity, not the Father's side. The negative, not the positive.

The mother does not only embrace her offspring with the arms of her affection, but she feeds it from the breasts of her consolation. Thus it is that whilst we are the offsprings of nature, and are dandled on her knees, she bountifully meets our numerous and diversified wants with profusion from her exhaustless stores.

The book is not presented to the reader in a form to be read from cover-to-cover. Its usefulness is yet further hindered by an *Index of*

Diseases which lists the names of the diseases under the plants used to treat them and, to make matters worse, the plants are not even listed in alphabetical order! Therefore, to find a particular disease or malady the reader is required to search plant-by-plant until he stumbles across it. To rectify this problem a new index has been prepared listing the plants alphabetically together with an entirely new cross-index listing the diseases and ailments alphabetically within four groups: *Physical, Mental, Spiritual* and what may be termed *Environemtal* (relationships with others, the world we live in — past and present, and behavioural problems). The groups should not be taken too rigidly as a degree of interchangeability must inevitably apply.

A further practical problem exists with the book which is that there lies lost within the various sections of individual plants, trees, shrubs, etc., some of Charubel's most important insights and explanations. This arrangement is indeed unfortunate and to aid the reader's overall understanding the following text (*The Natural World*) has been culled and assembled from within the body of the book.

THE NATURAL WORLD

Whatever may be said respecting the supernatural, there is nothing after all outside nature. What is nature but the workshop of the Infinite! Everything in nature is the subject of a force, and is also capable of transmitting a force. In the meantime not that identical force which it receives; simply because each subject becomes a chemical laboratory peculiarly its own, where, by virtue of those mysterious, because complicated, appliances it does generate another force, unlike that which it receives. I will illustrate this matter: An Alkaline substance becomes the recipient of an acid. What is the force generated? A Salt or a Saline. This Saline is unlike both of its factors.

The Infinite has innumerable hosts of agents in this great workshop, and the subjects of his power are just as innumerable. Each of these receive, through certain agencies, a force which comes from the Spirit Absolute, through the psychical. Seeing there is nothing higher than Spirit: God is a Spirit; there is nothing lower than what I call the objective material universe. And seeing these are all related, these are all within the domain of nature; where then lies the possibility for the supernatural?

I feel that the time is come for a systematic development of his most interesting branch of the Occult. It may be asked: Why I did not begin this work at an earlier date? My answer is: I had but scant sympathy in my struggles during the past; and it must be borne in mind that Psychics are sensitive, consequently, coldness, or even indifference, is but too quickly felt. Having recently had several very encouraging letters from a number of my subscribers in this country, America, and Australia; I am, in consequence, inspired with fresh vigour in the present work.

You have been made familiar with a portion of God's works in the domain of organic, and inorganic nature: Life under its numerous aspects accosts you at every turn, and from every point of view. There are none, whose experience is so contracted as to be shut out entirely, from a knowledge of some portion of animated nature. You are each acquainted with a number of the animals, and vegetables, which abound.

In the meantime, you are not so presumptuous as to fancy you have seen every plant, every flower, or every creature of every kind that live and move on the earth. You must know, that there are those who have seen more than you, yet, were you to ask the most advanced Naturalist if he had seen every species of animated nature, I feel certain his reply would be: However much I may have seen I have no reason to suppose that I have seen the whole; on the contrary, I have every reason to think I have not acquainted myself with but what lies on the outermost fringe, of that nature, whose limitations are unsearchable. This same holds true in every case, and would be admitted by Naturalist and Philosopher, as no one dare say that he has conversed with every class of animal life; every species of Infusoria; every form of insectorial existence; every crawling reptile; every quadruped; every biped; every bird of every plumage.

We are accustomed to call all mineral substances *inorganic matter*; in the meantime, such is not so in those primal formations which we discover among the mineral and metallic substances abounding in and on this earth. But when these substances are transformed by the hand of man, and their primitive structure broken up, the vital principle is no longer there, any more than the life principle remains in a tree when it has been cut up and transformed into chairs and tables.

The primal basis on which I build this new philosophy, if it may be called such, is: that every mineral substance, as well as every vegetable substance, has a living principle, soul, or genius;

and it is by virtue of this soul or genius that the stone is marked by certain characteristics, and contains certain properties, such as may be capable of acting on other substances or other organisms, and of producing changes in each.

This is my first thesis. My next is: that in order to become the subject of the influence, it is necessary we should become sympathetically connected with that stone, plant, or tree; not by first *killing* it and subsequently by taking portions in pills, powders, or decoctions; but by realising a sympathetic union with the stone, plant, or tree; and that by a kind of fascination, which you may designate love, towards that object. It is a law in nature, that whatever you *greatly* admire, and that, freely, or spontaneously, you love after a fashion; and what you love, or greatly admire, you become negative towards that object, and becoming thus negative, you must of necessity become receptive of whatsoever influences that thing may be capable of imparting.

It is well-known that you cannot force yourself to admire anything, but must be first of all fascinated by, or through, an inspiration. This inspiration is the precursor of fascination, and follows as the result of calm or quiet contemplation.

These are no idle fancies on my part, but are veritable truths. These are revelations which have been lying within the archives of the universe for thousands of years before our history awoke to meet the concurrent events of a time comparatively modern. We have straggling hints, or references, to peoples or nations who are said to have worshipped trees. Indeed some traces of such a kind of idolatry appears to be easily found among what are called the rude and barbaric tribes. These are but the remains of what was once a glorious philosophy.

There is not one within the shackled form of 'Old Mortality,' who may lay claim to this Omniscience. Such being the case, who dare to say that what I believe to exist is a myth?

There is that prejudice, arising from those teachings we have been indoctrinated with from our earliest days, by teachers, preachers, priests and parsons; that to die is the will of God.

In support of these we have those thousands of weeklies, monthlies, and quarterlies flowing from the press, the keynote of which is: "that it is appointed unto men once to die"; all preach death simply because the way to death is easier than it is to climb the steep and rugged path that leads to life.

I teach the way to life, and that at the risk of being called an Enthusiast, which I have been called by a latter-day-light. But such has been the fate of all who have dared to cut themselves adrift from that commonplace claptrap which is in vogue among the smart writers — so called — whose chief mission appears to be to laugh down the truth under every guise.

The false is the fashionable, and therefore the most popular among the currencies of this day. I tell you in my little sheet a truth which you may treat as you choose.

THE WORD OF GOD

Each plant on the Psychic Plane has a name, not, however, assigned capriciously by me, but, a name, that is the true and all-comprehensive one. This name is a *word*, and this word is the word of the Absolute, the one Universal Father! The Word of God is not confined to a book. Our Father's Big Book is Nature. His Word exists in every Herb, Plant and Tree.

The still voice of God in nature, which speaks to all alike, yet only a few attend to His teachings.

This word is an invocation of a mysterious but powerful nature. You will doubtless recognize in these characteristics, a striking resemblance, to one especial phrase connected with the pathological displays given by Jesus on more than one occasion. When unfolding the cryptic envelope, wherein was enclosed His Divine power, He made use of a WORD. A word which the onlooking multitude could hear, but which none of his listeners could interpret. When opening the ears of the deaf man He called aloud, yes, aloud, I know it was not a whisper: EPHPHATHA[†]. When raising the dead daughter of Jarius the Lord uttered forth that sublime word: TALITHA CUMI[‡]. Writers have pretended to furnish us with the interpretations of these words; but these interpretations are but guesswork. Do you suppose our Lord would have imposed a word on his nearest, and dearest friends which they could not understand, if He could otherwise have expressed himself? No. But He had a force yes a god to awake! to call forth an embodiment of a force necessary to give to those closed ears the capacity of

---

[†] MARK. 7:32–35 And they bring unto him one that was deaf, and had an impediment in his speech; and they beseech him to put his hand upon him. And he took him aside from the multitude, and put his fingers into his ears, and he spit, and touched his tongue; And looking up to heaven, he sighed, and saith unto him, Ephphatha, that is, Be opened. And straightway his ears were opened, and the string of his tongue was loosed, and he spake plain.

[‡] MARK. 5:38–42 And he cometh to the house of the ruler of the synagogue, and seeth the tumult, and them that wept and wailed greatly. And when he was come in, he saith unto them, Why make ye this ado, and weep? the damsel is not dead, but sleepeth. And they laughed him to scorn. But when he had put them all out, he taketh the father and the mother of the damsel, and them that were with him, and entereth in where the damsel was lying. And he took the damsel by the hand, and said unto her, Talitha cumi; which is, being interpreted, Damsel, I say unto thee, arise. And straightway the damsel arose, and walked; for she was of the age of twelve years. And they were astonished with a great astonishment.

17

hearing. The word which Jesus uttered bore some, resemblance to that word He uttered, when universal chaos vibrated with a new astonishment, when He spoke, and it was done; He commanded, and it stood fast. This word was not addressed to man. It was to secret, hence too sacred for man to understand. What I am here propounding is that there is a special word connecting itself with Nature's Divine Virtues, which when uttered awakes those forces into life and motion.

THE BODY AND SOUL

The Spirit has built up for itself this Spirit body which is called the soul, and by virtue of this inner body the outer body has been formed.

The inner body partakes of the semblance of the Immortal Spirit, and if this inner body continues in unison with the Spirit, which is called the I Am, it will itself become immortal, and will continue to be the temple of the Spirit, or the I Am! But if that soul or inner body revolts; if the psychic powers say we will not have this one to reign over us, it will forfeit its immortality; it then becomes broken up and diffused among its kindred element, and the Spirit returns to its fountain from whence it came, and that personality ceases to be. Consequently, for man to gain immortality he must "work out his own salvation," he must build up the inner house which is "his house from heaven."

Persons of gross habits, and where there may be a tendency toward vices of a low and animal character. Such persons may be relieved from an intolerable burden, a burden which if hugged and carried will ultimately weigh its possessor down to the gates of death. "For he who sows to the flesh, shall of the flesh reap corruption." And this corruption is the second death.

You may have read those words uttered by King David in one of his Psalms: "O spare me that I may recover strength before I go hence and be no more." It is evident that the Psalmist needed his soul strengthened. He must have had, for the time, a glimpse of another and interior body, which needed some little repairs before pulling down the old house. There was an epoch in the far past when man lived more on the psychic than on the so called intellectual plane; this is more than what the present humanity is capable of realising. Our present conceptions of beauty are not in unison with those possessed by man during one of those buried Æons of the past.

Nature closes each door after the birth of her offspring. Thus when one race has completed its round, fulfilled its mission, the door of that degree attained to by that race is closed behind it. The succeeding humanity cannot form any idea as to what may be the conceptions of its predecessor, but the predecessor may form correct notions of its successor. In the meantime, as there are always exceptions to every rule, or in other words, there ever have been those who have lived, whilst members of the succeeding race, the life of its predecessor, and have been able to realise what may have been the leading ideas of that race. But, when these exceptional characters seek to make these same ideas known to their contemporaries they are sure to be misunderstood, and what they say or write, for the time, will not be appreciated.

THE INTELLECT AND IMAGINATION

Some there are, who may consider these teachings as being but the wild hallucinations of an enthusiast; one who may be supposed to have been long a denizen in the domain of imagination, so as to have become intoxicated with those delusive dreams, which, like those fascinating exhalations which is said to have, at one time, ascended from the Pythian spring. But, what a sublime satisfaction it is to know that what the superficial thinkers, and writers, may understand by the epithet "imagination," as being equivalent to a vagary, the Occult Philosopher has made the very important discovery, that this tabooed region of imagination, is after all: the world, yes, the Universally Real.

The intellect alone, when uninspired, moves within a radius of a very contracted circle; and within these limits, the unaided intellect gets bewildered with those numerous enigmas which beset it on every hand.

After all those laborious researches, those testings and probings, and analytical siftings; when the diligent investigator is about to congratulate himself on his achievements, he may feel disposed to consider himself most fortunate, seeing he has attained to that long looked for consummation. In the midst of all this, he finds he has a successor, a rival, whose discoveries on those same lines, overturns the facts and theories of previous discoveries.

But the man whose intellect is illumined with the true light of heaven has no cause to fear that any one who may take up these same subjects on these same lines, will ever be in a position to say that what I have written is false. It is true, another mind may, at some future period appear on the scene, who may see more than I have seen, and who may express those lucid visions in loftier phrases.

CONCLUSION

I now approach the door, which opens at my call, and which conducts me toward a long yearned-for realization! The question I ask is this: Is there but one kind of means by which to prolong life on this earth, within the present body? Must all support of every kind pass through the ordinary process of mastication and digestion? It has been already shown, that to cure those various ills to which humanity are prone, it is not necessary that we should have resort to drugs and potions, taken by the mouth into the stomach. It has been already proved, since my first article on the *Psychology of Botany* appeared, that sicknesses may be cured by a look, accompanied by a thought directed towards a certain plant or tree, without the intervention of other means.

Such has been verified, and that by virtue of our higher nature coming in contact with that higher nature already alluded to, the lower nature may be cured. Do not such thoughts as these open the way, the true and living way, by which this outer nature may be preserved for any length of time? Most assuredly they do.

But here lie those obstacles, which, like those beings with wands of flame, who are said to guard the portal leading to the tree of life, are hard to surmount. There are accidents to which we are daily and hourly exposed. These consist of illness arising from exposure to those inclemencies which prevail in this our clime; arising chiefly from those accompaniments of artificial life, which are those leading characteristics of the present civilization, with which the present race is drenched to saturation.

We have our thousands of manufactories; each of which belches forth its portion of poisonous fumes. We have our large and thickly populated cities, each containing its background of slums, where live and die unseen, and unlamented teeming thousands, whose dwellings are dens of crime, and where reek those pollutions from whence do rise the "pestilence that walketh in darkness." These poisons permeate the purest atmosphere, nor is there any place out of their reach. Thus we are besieged by foes on every hand, besetting us at every turn through every lane of life. Under such conditions we find it very hard to counteract so many ills. I need not allude to those mechanical injuries to which this organism is open, and by which the present life might be cut off, or otherwise shortened, which at the time may have appeared of too trifling a nature to demand notice.

Then there are those numerous ills with which our nature may be tainted; those dire consequences of what our forefathers may have done, these all combined constitute a formidable army to fight and conquer in this our upward clambering toward the tree of life!

But there is yet another difficulty to contend with: that innate aversion, which abounds in the nature of the present race to all that may pertain to the psychic plane, of things unseen by mortal eyes, whilst at the same time manifesting an idolatrous devotion to the sensuous.

When pompous science has captured something new, its devotees make as much ado over the find as a young hen does over her first egg. At the same time, in many instances, such a discovery will never contribute the merest fraction towards making the race better, wiser, or happier. Do the multitude comprehend their sphere as perfectly as the Bee or the Ant? Intelligence is neither more nor less than the inspiration of the Almighty. This inspiration when beheld in the lower orders of creation you have been taught to denominate instinct; in man the same faculty you call intelligence, or inspiration.

Science seeks to attain to those hidden mysteries by its puerile researches, but hitherto without success, at least there have been no satisfactory results; for when partial success appears to have been achieved, some dire calamities have followed; nor will it ever be known the amount of evil that has been entailed by such; for if people persist on intruding into these domains; if presumptuous man will poach on the preserves of these conservative agents of nature's subtle forces, he must expect disaster. You readily may see that there is no new discovery of science, however promising its pretensions, but what has opened a door for fresh evils to visit and curse this earth. Pride and avarice are the two chief of devils that are making a hell of this once grand world, and these two are the inspirers and prompters in every new discovery, and in every fresh enterprise.

*   *   *   *   *

I, Charubel, am the ordained instrument to publish to this race, now to the sear of its life, this divine philosophy. However you may feel disposed to treat this subject, depend on it, there is no other messenger born, or yet within the folds of a distant future, who will publish again this philosophy further than he may seek to call the attention of the world to what I have written.

What I have written is written,

and will never be obliterated.

Charubel

Here then, O gentle reader, is Charubel's work presented anew — a unique guide to the spiritual essence of plants, minerals, and precious stones for the empathic healing of the physical body by the use of sigils, invocations, chants, aura, and the power of the will.

A. R. NAYLOR, 2003

Dedication

TO MY FAITHFUL AND SINCERE FRIEND, ROBERT WELCH, ESQ., to whom I leave all my works and manuscripts for publication, and use as articles for magazines, &c., &c., and also to my beloved and faithful wife, LILLY THOMAS, and to all kind friends who have helped and known me by my works, to the lovers of astrology, the occult arts, and those who strive for truth and justice.

THE PRESENT WORK IS A REVISED EDITION OF WHAT APPEARED IN THE *PSYCHIC MIRROR*, CONTRIBUTED SERIALLY, IS NOW PRESENTED TO THE INTELLIGENT PUBLIC AT THE REQUEST OF A FEW FRIENDS AND CHIEF supporters, who are of the opinion that a subject so unique — that is wonderful, at the same time profoundly philosophical, which by its applicability to the present state of the human race is deserving of universal acceptation, the same should be preserved in volume form. The thoughtful reader will discover that the *Psychology of Botany* and the *Psychology of Precious Stones*, combined, as they are, in the present volume, to be more, nor less than a complete system of occult philosophy. This philosophy is too expansive for the contracted steriotypic mind to accept; it is too profound for the "justices shallow" type to probe. The present work is a stranger, just appearing, as a revelation on this earth. Friends give my stranger a hearty welcome into your houses, on your bookshelf, and a place in your affections and by so doing oblige,

Yours ever faithfully,

CHARUBEL

THERE is an influence
emanating from each plant or
tree, and that when a person thinks
intently on any one of these, he, or
she, brings himself, or herself, in
sympathy with that plant or tree.

Introduction

ROM MY PSYCHOLOGICAL STANDPOINT I NOTE THERE IS A DIRECT SYMPATHY BETWEEN THE HUMAN SOUL, AND THE SOUL WHICH PERVADES, AND OCCUPIES EACH MEMBER — GREAT OR SMALL — OF THE VEGETABLE KINGDOM. IN THE MEANTIME I FAIL TO DISCOVER A SIMILAR SYMPATHY BETWEEN THE brute and the vegetable kingdom. This will, on first thought, appear to a great number of my readers, an anomaly, as the bovine tribes are more directly related to the vegetable, than what the human may appear to be. But, be it understood that the soul of the vegetable departs from the vegetable as soon as that organism is severed from its parent stem, or root, that is, the severed part. Hence, it follows, that a branch of a plant, or a part of its stem,

or, a part of its root has not the soul of that plant for pathological purposes when detached from its parent stem or root, nor is there any means yet discovered by which that subtle something called the soul may be captured.

Chemistry with its niceties, by way of analysis, or of synthesis, has hitherto failed to capture this most subtle, yet most potent element pervading the vegetable kingdom. There are no menstruums capable of dissolving the organic structure of a plant so quickly as to liberate the psychic principle and to capture it in its flight. It is therefore a thing impossible to find this potent factor in a dead organism. It is only with the soul in man, by the power of the will, supervised by celestial wisdom, that I have been able to achieve but a partial success in these my present researches. It is the recital of what has come under my own observation that will form the subjects of the present volume. At the same time, I shall not confine myself strictly, or slavishly, to that vocabulary in use among Orthodox Botanists.

As such scientific exactness is not necessary for the purpose I have in hand; what I am desirous of doing is, to point out in a practical manner, by inevitable tests, the one grand truth:— that there is a direct sympathy between the soul of a plant, and the human soul; and, further, that there is a *special* sympathy between certain plants and certain individuals, and, that man being the superior power, may control the soul force of the plant. Thus a man may, under certain conditions, grasp, or lay hold of the soul force of the plant, or tree, and procure the most occult properties of that vegetable, and apply them to his own personal uses, by way of healing himself of those ills, and infirmities of which he may be a victim. Or he may discover clairvoyantly what may apply to others.

What I am here stating is not a concocted jumble of extravagant notions, bearing but the merest semblance of rationality, not a wild theory, without a foundation to rest on, save being the baseless fabrication of an ever active fancy. On the contrary these matters have been tested by me in several instances, and that with astonishing results.

In the meantime I do not suppose for a moment that it is possible for *anyone* to practice this great and occult work, who tray not have developed those intuitional powers necessary to the finding of the vegetable plant, or tree, which the case might require.

To this very plant the soul of the initiated will be gradually drawn, and that as truly as that of the needle to the pole. But such results can never follow, where bias, or fancy is allowed to interfere by playing their round of delusive pranks. I will in this introduction give a few instances from the sphere of my own personal experience, by way of practically illustrating what is herein stated.

One day a friend of mine was suddenly seized with inward pains of a sharp pricking character in the lower part of the chest, extending down the left side. I was induced to place myself in a calm and tranquil condition — just as I am ever in the habit of doing, when in quest of a correct vision of any person subject or thing — saying to myself: I will look into the vast field of nature, "I have no crotchets, or preconceptions of my own to intercept from me the light of heaven," "I will look, yes, I will look." There must be a remedy for every ill, "the plaster must be as large as the wound." Such was my faith at that time, such is my faith at this day; and, so far as my experience goes on, has carried me hitherto, there is every probability that the future will find me much in advance of what I am this day.

I had not wandered far, nor waited long, before I saw a bush covered with yellow bloom resting on green foliage. At first I took this bush to be the Broom, but on closer inspection I found it to be the Gorse-bush, as soon as I made this discovery I realized an aura emanating from the bush of a brown colour, I united this aura with an aura which enveloped my patient, and within a quarter of an hour the pain was gone. A short time after this I had taken a severe cold, with pain in the ear; this pain was gradually becoming more severe. I looked in the same way as before. I had not looked long before I saw the MAIDENHAIR FERN, I manipulated the aura as before, and the pain in the ear left me and did not return.

Another case was that of a young girl who was suffering from extreme weakness accompanied with a cough, which, as it appears was the sequel of Scarlatina. This patient resided at the time in Cornwall. I looked as in the other cases, and the humble Lichen appeared the aura of which was gray mingled with red. This I applied a few successive days, suffice to say she was cured in a week. I was at that time testing some twenty more cases in the same way.

In these my allusions to my own experiences by way of testing the psychological virtues of various plants, with their magical powers, to eradicate those disorders to which our race are exposed, and to which they generally fall victims; I do not overlook the fact, that by far the majority are not SEERS, they are not endowed with CLAIRVOYANT abilities to guide them, and by which guidance they may discover those remedial agents in the vegetable kingdom, and that independently. This is why I came forward, as the champion representative of my fellow-men, by way of teaching every rational man or woman, how to act, or, how to think, so as to become the possessors of those valuable secrets, secrets that have never before been divulged, as I have made them known in the present volume. It is therefore necessary I should be explicit on all points, and convincingly clear to all that what I am publishing *is the truth*.

So far as I have been able to test the properties of Vegetables, whose virtues I have ascertained, in the first instance, by my introvisionary powers alone; and as all tests subsequently made, to prove the truth of this grand philosophy I am entitled to presume that those plants whose virtues, I am, by the force of circumstances, debarred a personal test, will notwithstandingly be accepted for true.

I shall, in the first instance, note the leading characteristics, and psychological properties of those common plants, with which the generality of my readers are more, or less, conversant. I shall treat of plants more or less progressively, as they appear to ascend in graduated degrees of development, and, not strictly as given by works on Botany.

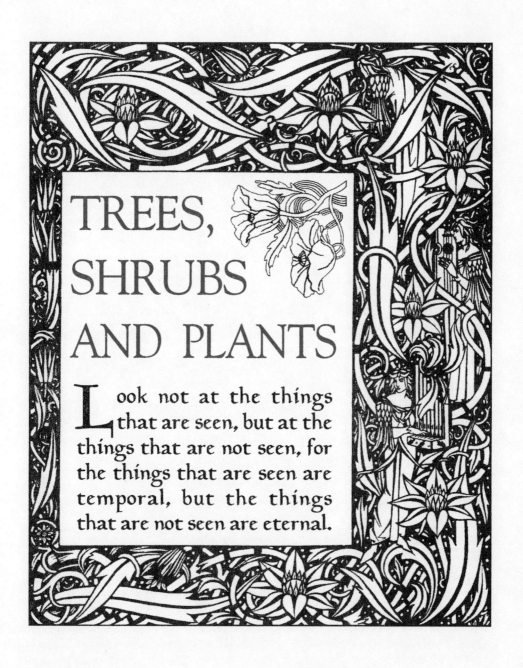

TREES, SHRUBS AND PLANTS

Look not at the things that are seen, but at the things that are not seen, for the things that are seen are temporal, but the things that are not seen are eternal.

THE LICHEN

THE FIRST VISIBLE SPECIES OF VEGETABLE LIFE IS THAT OF THE LICHEN. IT IS CONSEQUENTLY, THE FIRST SPECIES OF THE CRYPTOGAMIA CLASS, AND IS, IN TRUTH, THE FIRST AGENT MADE USE OF, BY NATURE'S LORD, AND LAW-GIVER, TOWARDS clothing the naked rocks, of new uprising islands. An island, as the result of an earthquake, may be ejected from the ocean depths within the short lapse of an hour. Not so is this the order observed by way of clothing its naked crags, and projecting rocks, and by which that island might become the home of animated life. The so called wilds of nature, as we witness them, at this day, were, at one time, in a very remote past, much wilder scenes; unsightly scenes of volcanic action; here and there a silenced crater, having choked itself, by its furious belchings. Today the once repulsive lava (if such an epithet be applicable to a period where, and when, nothing but silence could be the intermittent witness of such fury) is clothed with verdure, waving forests clothe those mountain sides; towns and villages securely rest in those lovely plains, plains, which at one time, were the scenes of one or more craters.

But we learn by observation, that counter forces, of various kinds, have been, and are, yet at work, since that time, and, amongst these agents the insignificant Lichen takes a foremost place. This fact goes to prove, that what the casual observer may designate *small* is, possibly, the greatest. Yes, that which man calls small, proves the greater in the eyes of its Maker. The Lichen performs its silent work on the naked rock, or aged stone wall, which the supposed mightier and more pretentious forces could never execute, simply by its clinging to its fixed abode, be it a stone, it overcomes a fractional portion of that stone, and, in time, the obduracy of the stone must yield to the operations of this silent grinder, and, in this way, prepare the first rudimentary particles of what we designate earth.

Longevity is one of the characteristics of the Lichen, but who by observation may learn its age! Who may note the mystic hour of its birth? We know that its first germs must have been wafted by the winds from its hiding places in the higher atmospheric region, having floated about in search of a place waiting its mysterious advent; that place was one which would not attract any other than the Lichen:– a naked rock or an exposed stone wall; here it is doomed to live, here it must labour, here it builds its own dwelling, and here it makes its own grave, but of its ashes its more mature successor develops, and continues, the labours of its predecessor. This again, in the course of centuries dies, and bequeaths to the rock the fruits of its labour, which is its own defunct organism. Each successive worker leaves the field a little in advance of its predecessor. Yet the keenest observer of one generation may fail to perceive the shadow of a change, and, when a Lichen dies, who may perceive the change of the unaided human eye? The Lichen wears the garb of immutability! My readers will know the little Lichen readily, that thin, hard, gray crust which may be seen on an old large or small stone or rock; a growth requiring for its support but the light of the sun with the surrounding atmosphere.

I am not aware of the Lichen being a medicinal vegetable, beyond this; that it is of a flowerless class, the *Cryptogamia*. And as such is one of the predecessors of the Liverwort, the virtues of which may be partially known to medical Botanists. On the Psychic Plane, however I am conversant with its great powers, or virtues, to control and conquer the following complaints:– Leprosy, Scaly Skin Diseases, a particular Poison in the Blood, such as often follows Scarlatina

THE REMEDY:– This is not found in pills, tinctures, or decoctions; but is found on the Psychic Plane. The cure is effected by the sight of a symbol, and the utterance of a word.

This is the sigil

╟──O──╢

of the Lichen.

The word for invocation is

BATH—RA—EL.

Let the person who may be suffering from a complaint
corresponding to one of those stated above, go into a room alone.
Let him, or her fix his eyes on the sigil, and deliberately, and
sacredly utter the word BATH-RA-EL ten times, allowing about
one minute to lapse between each utterance. This should be
done between the hours of ten, and midnight. As to posture,
sit; or stand; or kneel; as you may feel disposed to act; or which
posture might be the most agreeable, for most convenient.

THE MOSSES

THERE MAY BE AS MUCH BEAUTY IN THE STRUCTURAL FORMATION OF THE MOSSES, AS MAY BE RECOGNIZED ABOUNDING IN OR AMONG, THE LARGER MEMBERS OF THE VEGETABLE KINGDOM. THERE ARE BUT FEW — COMPARATIVELY SPEAKING — WHO HAVE RECEIVED THE EDUCATION NECESSARY FOR MINUTE, OR, scientific observation; through the lack of which much of that beauty, and, otherwise, captivating loveliness to them is lost; but, beyond this, and what opposes progress in these Botanical researches, is *apathy*, or the lack of interest, on the part of the public towards these studies.

I will give in this place, a few of those characteristics among the Mosses, such as may be seen by an ordinary person without scientific attainments. First of all, I would remark, that there are some, which are called Moss, which are more allied to the *Lichens*. We have one which is called Iceland Moss, but which is evidently a species of *Lichen*, and allied to the Liverwort. This has medicinal properties which are well known, whose decoctions are of value as a Pulmonary. There is an "Irish Moss," which is not a true Moss. Both of these so called Mosses are gelatinous. The true Moss is not. Secondly the true moss is always green except when dried up; the *Lichen* is, invariably, more grey than otherwise. Thirdly, Mosses are endowed with a kind of stem, round which minute leaves are arranged, with admirable regularity; at the same time, the stem is not woody. This is not so with the *Lichen*.

Although the true Moss be — so far as my knowledge extends — void of medicinal properties, psychologically, it is capable of producing marvels. I here give one instance: which is recorded of Mungo Park,[†] the African traveller. "This enterprising traveller during one of his journeys into the interior of Africa was cruelly stripped, and robbed of all that he possessed, by banditti." In this forlorn and almost helpless condition, he says, "when the robbers had left me, I sat for some time, looking around me in amazement and terror. Whichever way I turned nothing appeared but danger, and difficulty. I found myself in the midst of a vast wilderness, in the depth of the rainy season — naked and alone — surrounded by savage animals, and by men still more savage. I was five hundred miles from any European settlement. All these circumstances crowded at once

† I am indebted for this account to Wm. Carpenter M.D., F.R.S., work on *Vegetable Physiology*.

upon my recollection, and I confess that my spirits began to fail me. I considered my fate as certain, and I had no alternative but to lie down and perish. The influence of religion, however, aided and supported me. I reflected that no human prudence, or foresight could possibly have averted my present sufferings. I was indeed a stranger, in a strange land, yet I was still under the protection of that providence who has condescended to call Himself the Stranger's Friend. At this moment, painful as my reflections were, the extraordinary beauty of a small Moss, irresistibly caught my eye, and, though the plant was not larger than the top of one of my fingers, I could not contemplate the delicate conformation of its roots, leaves, and fruit, without admiration. Can that Being (thought I) who planted, watered, and brought to perfection, in this obscure part of the world a thing, which appears of so small importance, look with unconcern upon the sufferings of creatures after His own image? Surely not — Reflections like these would not allow me to despair. I started up, and disregarding hunger, and fatigue, travelled forward, assured that relief was at hand — and I was not disappointed." I desire to make a very important remark relative to this incident. In the first place, the courage of this traveller had been completely subdued, he had become passive, and in his weakness he made a discovery—a little Moss! The same kind as I am now presenting to my readers. Mungo Park looked on it until admiration ended in love. He loved that bit of Moss. He thus became in sympathy with the genius of the Moss, and thus attracted to his aid a power surpassing that of mortal! If any of my readers could but love as Mungo Park did, he would find a helping hand in trouble. The little ones, have angels, who behold the face of the Father.

The infirmities, for which the Moss — psychologically — is an antidote, are Vagaries, False, or Delusive Visions; Hallucinations of every kind; Despondency; Melancholy of every cast; and Suicidal Proclivities.

Any one afflicted, with one or more of the above-named evils, may find deliverance through psychological sympathy with the Moss; under the following conditions:—

This is the sigil 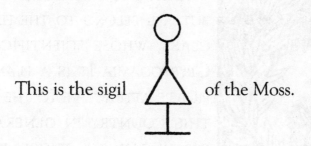 of the Moss.

The word for invocation is

AR—RUT—EL.

Fix your eyes on the Sigil. If you can realize the Moss itself, as well, do so. Look on this Sigil, or on the Moss, (*the living* Moss), not a bit plucked up or detached from its place, for a few minutes before speaking the word. Then utter the word distinctly, and sacredly seven times; allow a minute, between each word.

THE FERNS (*Filices*)

THERE ARE SEVERAL SPECIES OF THE FERN BUT ALL BELONG TO THE FLOWERLESS CLASS, WHOSE SCIENTIFIC NAME IS CRYPTOGAMIA IT IS A PLANT WHICH PROVES ATTRACTIVE TO THE PEOPLE OF THIS COUNTRY IN GENERAL; MORE ESPECIALLY TO THOSE WHO ARE ENDOWED WITH A MODICUM OF TASTE, ACCOMPANIED WITH A LOVE OF NATURE, UNDER HER MANY GUISES. WHY IS THIS SO? I THINK IF THERE WERE NOTHING more attractive, than the outward arrangement of its leaves; the formation and colour of its stem; or the odour arising from its foliage —which may be considered by some more oppressive than pleasing — even people of taste, education, and refinement, could not find in so unpretentious a plant, so much to admire. But here lies the grand secret: there is a play of forces — forces which arise from, or through, the Fern, and which play on the nerves of its admirers, even to fascination.

The nature of the aura which proceeds from the Fern is not exciting, hence its action on the nerves of its lovers is non-stimulative but rather a sedative, accompanied with a pleasant coolness, which tends to tone down the too excitable condition of the brain. Hence it happens, that most excitable people, as a rule, manifest the greater amount of admiration, and sympathy for the Fern. This is the still voice of God in nature, which speaks to all alike, yet only a few attend to His teachings.

I cannot advise people of a cold, and melancholic temperament, to pay much attention to this cold and sombre plant, further than as it may fall in with their studies, as its remedial influence, would not prove of benefit to them. In these remarks I am simply alluding to Ferns in general I will, however, now descend to particulars and treat of that species designated generally.

WALL FERN

THE CLASSIC NAME OF WHICH IS *POLYPODIUM* THIS LITTLE PLANT MAY BE READILY DISTINGUISHED FROM OTHER SPECIES OF FERN, BY ITS SHORT UPRIGHT LEAF-STALK, WHICH SHOOTS UP FROM AN HORIZONTAL STEM, WHICH STEM CREEPS ALONG THE GROUND, ON, OR NEAR THE SURFACE. THIS SPECIES MAY BE FOUND ON old mossy dikes; but more especially about the decayed stems of old defunct oaks. The leaves are attractively arranged opposite each other. The aura which I perceive emitting from this lovely plant, is, deep green with a nimbus of golden surrounding like a border. The phenomenon is captivating! The Soul of the Wall Fern is in sympathy with the human heart, that is: it is a heart strengthener. It acts powerfully, yet not disturbingly, on the arterial system, and more, or less beneficially on all chest affections arising from weakness. Those residing in the country where this species abounds, who may be suffering from weak action of the heart, or Atrophy (general weakness with wasting) would act wisely by visiting this little plant in its native state, look intently at it for some time as your state, or condition, permits; *but do not mutilate the plant, or remove it from its primitive condition*, for psychological purposes.

This is the sigil

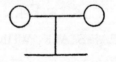

of the WALL FERN (*Polypodium*).
The word for invocation is ARU-EL

The ritual to be observed is as follows:—Take thy stand, afflicted one, face toward the sun, or place of the sun, ten minutes before noon, within doors, or out of doors. If too feeble to stand, sit, if unable to sit, lie; but let thy face be toward the sun at noon, but be in your place ten minutes before noon. Then and there repeat the following:—

Revolving earth, behold yon sun!

My wants are great, my God is one,

The stars are countless as they shine,

They say they'll cure those ills of mine.

Great Lord of Light—with awe I speak;

My heart does fail — I am so weak,

My star of hope, is in this word!

ARU-EL — ARU-EL — my God! my Lord!

Observe. Go through this ritual till well.

THE ADDER'S TONGUE.
(*Ophioglossum*)

THE AURA OF THIS SPECIES OF FERN, IS OF A VERY DARK GREEN HUE, WITH A TINGE OF PURPLE. THE PSYCHICAL PROPERTIES OF THIS SPECIES OF FERN ARE MARVELLOUS; BUT, FOR THE PRESENT, MANY OF ITS PROPERTIES ARE INVOLVED IN MUCH THAT IS OBSCURE, AND MYSTICAL; WHICH, however, is destined, eventually to evolve into the light. I here allude to what is not, as yet, been made known to me. I will in the meantime give to the reading and studious public what has been made known to me. The aura, or Psychic influence of this plant, is antidotal to numerous baneful influences; influences, given out by evil disposed men, with the intention of injuring their fellow-men; which proceedings are designated *Black Magic*. There are men, and women, on this earth, at the present day; who are guilty of murder, who, in the meanwhile, escape the murderer's righteous doom. These go unpunished, because the legislators of this, and other countries, ignore the truth of all such allegations as I am making; consequently such characters may safely go on in their diabolical work. But, thanks to God, and His angelic hosts, the dark ones have it not all their own way. As there are those who have the power to curse; so there are a few who have the power to bless. These blessings are no shams.

Every radical complaint has its seat in the soul. It is here that the primal germ of every complaint is deposited; it is here it develops its true characteristics, in and through the bodily functions, by which the nature of the disease is determined.

Evil influences from persons with evil intent develop through that organ called the spleen. In this way that grand reservoir of life force becomes poisoned, and the free action of this organ becomes impeded. This condition of the spleen, makes the afflicted one conscious of sensations, not hitherto having experienced. The sufferer finds himself less energetic, his accustomed cheerfulness subsides, a general torpor pervades him; his usual interest he took in the matters of daily life, gives place to listless apathy. Life becomes a burden. His medical attendant seeks, but seeks in vain, for the cause. Death ensues.

I find I had not stated in the *Psychic Mirror*, clearly, how the Adder's Tongue was to be applied; I shall now make all clear, and that to my readers' advantage.

This is the sigil

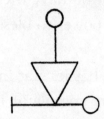

of the Adder's Tongue.

The word for invocation is

VI–VOO–EL.

Take your stand with face to the east, and right hand pointing heavenward about the hour of sunrise. Repeat this invocation slowly three times over.

The Invocation

Great Light of light! dispeller of my gloom!
Giver of life, and emptier of the tomb,
My night is past! the dawn I see quite well,
'Tis day! 'tis day! my mighty VI–VOO–EL.

MARES-TAIL *(Hippuris)*

BOOKS DEVOTED TO MEDICAL BOTANY, GIVE BUT LITTLE INFORMATION AS TO THE MEDICINAL PROPERTIES OF THIS PLANT. THEY MAY BE FOUND GROWING PLENTIFULLY IN, OR NEAR STAGNANT POOLS, AND, IN MARSHY, OR SWAMPY PLACES IN THIS LAND. THERE ARE, HOWEVER, CHEAP BOOKS IN THE MARKET, DEVOTED TO DESCRIPTIVE BOTANY, I CONSIDER IT needless, I should waste time, and occupy space, on such a line when the same might be purchased at a bookstall. I shall confine myself to what cannot be purchased otherwise than by reading my revelations. This is my mission to impart.

On the soul plane, *Hippuris* appears far more beautiful, than it does in its present uninviting form of earthly guise; but such may be truly said of every plant, save this, that the disparity between the two states appear greater — as in the present instance — than with others. In the present instance the vision I have of the Psychic *Hippuris* is as follows:– Its hue is that of a much lighter, and much brighter green than that of its present aspect, more especially is this so just about the stem, more so than the leaves, or whirl which surround the stem. An aura surrounds the whole plant — nimbus-like — of a deep dark purple; a colour which impresses one with the idea that some mystical properties abound in the sphere of the Mares-tail. Medical Botanists affirm this plant to be a weak astringent; at the same time they consider it inferior to other, and safer, remedies. I am prepared to admit this to a certain extent. In the meantime, I feel convinced that this plant — psychically — may be applied to uses which no other plant may serve. One of these uses, I dare to mention: an *Anti-fat*. The undue deposit of fat in the human, is a disease; the absorbents do not perform their work efficiently; hence, the secretion of fatty matter is the spontaneous consequence. Fat, in my view, is a species of dross, a kind of waste matter, and a burden to the mortal who has to carry it. I am here alluding to the unnecessary fat. I write on this subject feelingly from personal experience, and, although I may not compare with thousands suffering from obesity; at the same time I know rather more of this complaint than is agreeable.[†]

It will be seen, that when this appeared for the first time in the *Psychic Mirror*, I had not got the sigils of those plants, which are alluded to, I had not at that period advanced far enough; it

---

† I am greatly reduced since that time.

is true, I had partially, and to a very limited extent developed; hence it is that while I got the sigils of a few plants and trees, there were several of the *Cryptogamia* class as well as a few of others I had not attained to. I am at present in a condition to be able to procure the sigil, or symbol, of each plant or tree whose character I may seek to give. I gave advice as to how to procure the virtues of the Mares-Tail but the advice then given, fell far short of being satisfactory. There is no advice complete, apart from the sigil. In order to cross a river, from one side to the other, you must have a boat or a bridge. The sigil is that bridge by which you may come in touch with the virtues of the plant or tree.

The soul of the afflicted one suffers sympathetically with the bodily infirmity, in that it was the soul which suffered first, and from its psychic state that suffering penetrated, and permeated, the physical body. As before stated, the plant called Mares-Tail is the cure for obesity; seeing such a provision is made, through this plant, what may be that special power, property, or virtue, exercised by the genius of this plant? The answer is, that of counteracting interceptional obstacles, and thus producing a regulated currency, in, and through, every duct, capillary, or channel, which may permeate the whole of the human system. But to do this work effectively the sigil must be discovered by me, and recorded for your inspection; accompanied by the invocative word.

This is the sigil

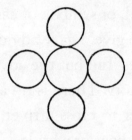

of the Mares-Tail.

The word for invocation is

EL—NE—RAH.

Repeat this word over four times between the hours of 9:00 and 11:00 at night; with both hands down by your side, and eyes directed to the ground. On the Physical Plane, plants have their names, and these names are founded on some peculiarity characteristically of that class to which these plants belong. Hence the name is intended to convey to the mind of the student a correct idea respecting some of those leading characteristics by which that particular plant might be distinguished from thousands of others. Even so, each plant on the Psychic Plane has a name, not, however, assigned capriciously by me, but, a name, that is the true and all-comprehensive one. This name is a *word*, and this word is the word of the Absolute, the one Universal Father! The Word of God is not confined to a book. Our Father's Big Book is Nature. His Word exists in every Herb, Plant and Tree.

THE ASH TREE (*Fraxinus*)

THIS TREE IS SAID TO BE A MEMBER OF THE OLIVE TRIBE. MANY VIRTUES ARE ASCRIBED TO THIS TREE BY MEDICAL BOTANISTS; AND AMONG OTHERS, IT IS SAID TO BE AN *ANTIBILIOUS* MEDICINE; FOR WHICH PURPOSE THE POWDERED BARK IS USED, AND IN DECOCTION. IT ACTS ON THE LIVER BENEFICIALLY. VIEWED FROM THE PSYCHIC PLANE; this tree has a purple, or deep plum colour, which grows darker towards the ends of the branches. The lower part of the stem is a beautiful mauve. Such is the Ash Tree as beheld by me on the soul-plane. There is one very marked peculiarity connected with this phenomenal display: the branches end, in what resembles a very dark fog; by which I learn, that the leaves, and outermost branches, even, in its earthly garb, possess subtle properties; not to be found in the bark, or the lower part of the stem. It is a well-known fact, as recognized by those living in rural districts, that rain droppings falling from the leaves of the Ash Tree kills all vegetation which may aspire to live beneath its shades. I here approach the main subject, to which every observation is, or should be, subservient, which is, the healing properties, on the Psychologic Plane: Acute Pain in the Chest, or affections of the Bronchia — the result of obstruction. Let the sufferer direct his, or her thoughts to the stem of the Ash Tree. But by way of rendering further assistance to the afflicted one, who may be seeking the remedy; I here give the sigil, or symbol of the Ash Tree, which expresses the mystical powers, properties, or virtues, of the tree.

This is the sigil 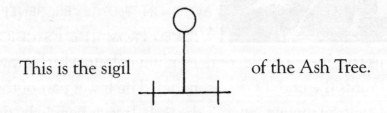 of the Ash Tree.

The word for invocation is

HOO-MEL

You imbibe, by faith, the aura, drink in by your inspirational desires this Divine Remedy. This remedy promotes the various secretions that may be obstructing, in this way this remedial agency aids nature, by carrying away various impurities. Beyond all this, the leaves and outermost branches, contains a safe, and sure remedy for Tumours, Abscesses, and all Chronic Excrescences of the Skin. When such a treatment is required, direct your thoughts, as intently as possible, to the green leaves, *in your mind;* but as it may not be possible to see an Ash Tree where you may chance be situated, therefore, in the absence of the tree, you may contemplate this symbol, which is the key that unlocks the door, which opens, and admits you into those mysteries which may help you, in the absence of your knowledge of the why's and wherefore's.

But, additional to all this, I have hitherto said; I hold in my grasp a CELESTIAL EXPRESSION, a silent one. The symbol is an expression, and is far louder than any vocalised one; for the organ of human speech is incapable of uttering, what this symbol utters. But this word celestial, embodies the forces you need, and, which at the time, places an instrument in your reach, by use of which you may command the needful forces, and they will forthwith come and obey you. But, some one will here reply: What! Am I asked to use a word, whose meaning is hidden from me? My answer to thy question is:–If thou rejectest all but what thy intellect may be able to grasp, and subsequently hold, and retain; then, I must confess, thy sphere is a narrow one, thy prospects cheerless, and thou art poor indeed; but, if thou insistest on an explanation, I have none to give, beyond what has already been given.

I need not reiterate my former injunctions, with respect to that reverential mood of mind to be observed in the use of the Word here given. You may use it as often as prompted, until the benefit you are anticipating be a realized fact. Choose for yourself the most convenient time. In all cases, have the sigil before your eyes, and, what with the contemplation of what you are looking on, conjoined with the word utterance, you will in a short time realize wonders.

BROOK-LIME *(Veronica-Beccalinga)*

THE POPULAR NAME OF THIS PLANT IS BROOK-LIME. BEING A PLANT SO GENERALLY KNOWN, BY THOSE WHO RESIDE IN RURAL DISTRICTS; I CONSIDER MANY WORDS, BY WAY OF DESCRIPTION, UNNECESSARY BEYOND THIS: IT IS A SUCCULENT LITTLE PLANT WHICH GROWS plentifully by watercourses in secluded, or shady places, and is, generally, a companion of that well-known, and highly valued plant the WATERCRESS. Medical Botanists hold up this plant as an antiscrobutic, and blood purifier, hence a remedy for Jaundice, and all Kidney Complaints. But in all its applications, the green plant, or its juice, should be used.

Such is a brief outline of the virtues of this little plant, in its material form on this earth plane. My work, however, is on the other side of nature. Meantime, I do not ignore the natural properties of this plant, by referring to that which surpasses the natural, viz.: the *supernatural*. I simply open another door, leading out of the seen into the unseen, out of body into soul. My mission is not to diminish, but to enhance the virtues of the plants and trees which come under my observation. I shall therefore look into this little plant very minutely, and that from a psychic point of view. What I see is a light green mist surrounding the plant, extending but a few inches beyond, or above it, holding the shape of the plant in all its conformations.

Its Antedotal Virtues

The parts of the body for which the psychic plant is in direct sympathy are the Spinal Chord, and Lower Brain, also the nerves of nutrition generally. Anyone afflicted with Spinal Irritation; Restlessness; Sleeplessness; accompanied with a dead ache in the head; apply the remedy by thinking intently on the plant; and, go over the Invocative term, looking intently, and steadfastly, on the symbol as given below.

This is the sigil

of the Brook Lime.

The word for invocation is

ATH–RU–EL.

Go through this ritual, when you may feel the need
of help Divine, and that as often, as you may feel
prompted.

There are but few, I think, that will fail to
comprehend enough of these teachings, so as to derive
the needed benefit, ease, and comfortable rest; as the
remedy is not reluctantly given, but is waiting on your
receptivity.

THE LILAC *(The Olive Tribe)*
BOTH THE ASH, AND THE LILAC BELONG TO THE OLIVE TRIBE, NOTWITHSTANDING THE GREAT DISSIMILARITY IN THEIR OUTER CONFORMATION AS SEEN BY THE UNSCIENTIFIC OBSERVER.

The Lilac is a shrub familiar to nearly every person — not blind, and who may have attained his, or her majority, and being in full possession of, but the ordinary faculties requisite for observation. The fragrance of the bloom is sweet. I have much to say of this plant — psychically — notwithstanding the silence of the Medical Botanists, as to the virtues of the Lilac on the soul plane. In the first place, I have discovered the one, and most prominent complaint to which this plant applies, sympathetically, from its psychic plane of existence, is a certain affection of the heart, where the action is too quick, and, in the meantime, too feeble. Such a case came under my observation some time back. The person in question had been afflicted with this complaint for several years — off and on — but, more especially, when the subject of undue excitement, or worry. Recently the complaint had become considerably worse. I felt sorry for the sufferer and being pressed for a remedy I directed my thoughts to the soul world, this being my final resource. At once the Lilac came to view. I applied a leaf from the psychic tree, and strange — yes, wonderful to relate — the heart became calm, the oppressive, feelings departed, and refreshing sleep followed. I am able to affirm the old distressing sensations have not returned.

What I have here stated is a fact, I relate this in ordinary language; there being no attempt, on my part, to mystify in the least. Yet such is the apathy of people generally, and even of sufferers themselves, by way of adopting such measures as I am here recommending that I am disposed to despair of finding but few, out of all my readers, who will accept of my gratuitous advice as to this celestial remedy; it being otherwise more probable, that, like the Syrian General, when advised by the Prophet to submerge his body seven times in Jordan in order he might be cured of his Leprosy; went away in a rage; and why? Simply that the remedy was not encumbered sufficiently with what should have been an imposing ritual.

The soul aura of the Lilac is a strengthener and sustainer of the life principle in the human body. This aura is of a lustrous golden hue. There is a word allied to the psychic potencies, connected with the Lilac.

The word for invocation is

EPH–LE–HI–MAH

This word is an invocation of a mysterious but powerful nature. You will doubtless recognize in these characteristics, a striking resemblance, to one especial phrase connected with the pathological displays given by Jesus on more than one occasion. When unfolding the cryptic envelope, wherein was enclosed His Divine power, He made use of a WORD. A word which the onlooking multitude could hear, but which none of his listeners could interpret. When opening the ears of the deaf man He called aloud, yes, aloud, I know it was not a whisper: EPHPHATHA. When raising the dead daughter of Jarius the Lord uttered forth that sublime word: TALITHA CUMI. Writers have pretended to furnish us with the interpretations of these words; but these interpretations are but guesswork. Do you suppose our Lord would have imposed a word on his nearest, and dearest friends which they could not understand, if He could otherwise have expressed himself? No. But He had a force yes a god to awake! to call forth an embodiment of a force necessary to give to those closed ears the capacity of hearing. The word which Jesus uttered bore some, resemblance to that word He uttered, when universal chaos vibrated with a new astonishment, when He spoke, and it was done; He commanded, and it stood fast. This word was not addressed to man. It was to secret, hence too sacred for man to understand. What I am here propounding is that there is a special word connecting itself with Nature's Divine Virtues, which when uttered awakes those forces into life and motion. The psychic dynamical word for the Lilac is EPH-LE-HI-MAH. I divide the word into its literal syllabic form, for the purpose of distinctness of expression. Heart affections are very prevalent in these days of high pressure, in all business vocations; such being the recognized order of the day.

As an antidote, I present you with the psychologic virtues of the Lilac, including a few necessary remarks by way of instruction.

1. Banish from your mind all existing prejudices; forget for a while — at least — the old hackneyed word "superstition"; and, for awhile, ignore your scientifical superiority, and crotchety foibles.

2. Select a time during the twenty four hours when you may calculate on having quiet, and, of being quiet.

3. Discharge from your thoughts the business matters of the day.

4. Direct your thoughts to the Lilac-bloom or branch. Repeat the word six times and look on the symbol.

This is the sigil

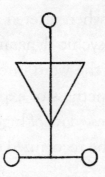

of the Lilac.

The word for invocation is

EPH—LE—HI—MAH.

DEVIL'S BIT (*Scabiosa Succisa*)
THIS LITTLE HERB GROWS PROFUSELY
AND PLENTIFULLY IN OLD PASTURES,
IN ALL PARTS OF THIS COUNTRY. THE
FLOWER IS OF A DULL BLUE SHADE,
HARD, AND ROUND. THE STEM IS
HARD AND TOUGH, GROWING FROM
ONE TO TWO FEET HIGH. THE ROOT
is fibrous, and, appears as if one part had been recently bitten
off, by some animal. Hence the comic tradition, that the reputed
enemy of mankind, knowing of the valuable properties of this
plant, enviously bit off a portion of the root.

From what is here related, you may infer that this plant must
be endowed with strange potencies.

The psychic virtues of this notorious herb, differ widely from
those given in its earthly dwelling, by the Naturalists. There
are few points alike between the two states, or in harmony. For
as it is with the human personality who differs, considerably, on
the other side to what he appeared to be on this earth side of
life. Even so is it with vegetables. Some very humble plants,
like the one in question, has a far lovelier foliage, and a more
attractive bloom on the soul plane than it has at present. This
plant is much larger, more highly developed, and its colours
more variegated.

In the meantime, what I see in respect of appearances is of but secondary value, but what may be the pathological properties of this plant is of the greatest importance to mankind. This plant, like several others of the vegetable tribes, is one of many virtues, virtues far more numerous than the Botanists of the past ever surmised, or dreamed of. The virtues I am alluding to, are the psychical, and not the physical; hence the practical use, or application of those virtues are effected in one and the same way as in all other herbs, plants or trees.

These applications may be effected by proxy. You may heal, or restore another, for whom you sympathise, and that without the knowledge of the individual, or the exercise of the will of the afflicted one.

I will here point out, one other terrible affliction for which this plant, if rightly applied, is the antidote. It is what I designate, a soul blight; the result of psychic parasites!

But, as further dilations would involve what would be imprudent to make known in any publication, I shall here close the subject.

This is the sigil

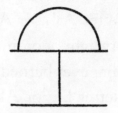

of the Devil's Bit.

The word for invocation is

MO–RU.

THE OAK (*Quercus Robur*)
AS THIS TREE IS OF EVERY NATION, OF EVERY CLIME AND OF EVERY AGE, THE TREE OF RENOWN; I SHALL TREAT OF EVERY PARTICULAR CONNECTED WITH THE OAK ELABORATELY, AND EXTENSIVELY. IN DOING JUSTICE TO THIS GREAT TREE, I SHALL confine my remarks, and observations, within the bounds, or limitations, of authentic literature. To accomplish this object, I shall give the radical name of this tree by which it was known at the infancy of history and as described in the most venerable

records of a hoary antiquity. In the Hebrew Bible this tree is designated Ashel. The root of this name is supposed to be Gashel. The Hebrew letter Ash, or *AS,* conveys the idea of light, or fire; not ordinary light or ordinary fire; but, that primal light, and first of fires, that ever burned, before the light of day, or dawn of time. The letter EL, or AL, ever alludes to those primal powers, or celestial intelligences, whose residence is the entire ambient: that region in which revolve the sun, and moon, and all the host of heaven. The EL stands for what, in the Hebrew tongue, signifies the gods, thus when the two letters are joined — ASH-EL, whose literal translation into English would be the god-fire, or god-light, as the letter Ash would bear either the *light* signification, or the *fire* interpretation; but the latter appears the more correct. Such being the radical idea which the name of this tree conveys in the Hebrew language. There is another idea which is applicable to the Oak, but in the meantime, is to be taken only in a secondary sense, that is *Defender,* or *Mediator.* We are consequently naturally led to conclude with the question that finding the Hebrew language attaches such an idea to the Oak; is there any authentic records of the Hebrew nation giving to the Oak divine honours? Yes, verily, we have such a record in no less an authority than the Hebrew Bible. I shall point out, by way of reference, a few passages having a direct bearing on this subject. In the 21st chapter of Genesis, it is thus recorded: "And Abraham planted a grove in Beer-sheba, and called there on the Lord, the everlasting God." This grove consisted of Oak exclusively, and was not a mixed class of trees on the fashion of the modern parks which are to please the eye. This grove could not have been for the luxury of salubrious shade, as the young plants could not have attained such dimensions in the lifetime of the patriarch. In the 31st chapter of the 1st Samuel we have an account of the bones of Saul and his sons being buried under an Oak, in Jabesh-Gilead, after being cremated. But the Bible student will be familiar with other passages of a like order, giving unmistakable proofs of the Oak being regarded as a sacred tree in the earliest ages or times of Hebrew history. Additional to the sacred records, I will refer you to what is designated, by way of distinction, *profane history*. Here we have an account of Romulus opening a famous Asylum between two groves of Oak. In the early days of Greece we learn of the famous oracle of Jupiter, at the Oaks of Dodana. Among both Greeks and Romans we find the Oak set apart as sacred to Jupiter. But it was in Britain where Oak was pre-eminently adored in the far past, by our forefathers, the ancient Britons, as related in their feasts and festivals. More especially the grand annual festival which answers to our Christmas-tide, and from which our Christmas has been borrowed. As Jupiter, who owns this tree, is said to be the father of the gods, even so is the Oak, the king among trees. The Oak being the tree of Jupiter could not be otherwise than sacred in the estimation of the devotional Briton. Nor is that reverence yet extinct; no, it is not altogether a thing belonging to a mythic past, as, to my knowledge, there are a few in this country, at this day, who pay more than ordinary reverence to this tree of millenniums! We are led to suppose, by the Ministers and Priests of Modern Christianity that the reverence which the Druids, among the Britons paid the Oak, was idolatry. If they were idolaters then are the Ministers and Priests of a meaningless ritual idolaters.

Why that reverence for a building made with hands? Why those attitudinal changes, or genuflections, in the presence of decorative art, or ephemeral ornamentation? If these deserve being called sacred; how much more sacred those sombre shades, afforded by those ample bows of this father, and king of the forest trees. The Oak, as already stated, is the tree of Jupiter. Jupiter as estimated by Astrologers is the largest and greatest benefit of all the plants in the Solar System. In the meantime, Jupiter, as regarded by sages of Prehistoric times, Jupiter was the King of Space, and Director of the Forces of Nature. Jupiter was the representative of the one true God in the classic history of the Greeks and the early Roman Age. Thus we find the one grand festival of the Druids was celebrated at the time of the Winter Solstice; that is when the sun, by apparent motion enters Capricorn. When the sap of trees begin to ascend. It is here we find the Christian Fathers, in order to reconcile the supposed heathen to the new religion, turned this festival to be the commemoration of another sun: the "Sun of Righteousness."

Everything belonging to the Oak was held sacred. Hence the Mistletoe that grew on the Oak was held in the highest veneration by the Druids on the day the sun entered Capricornus, or rather when it came to that point designated the Winter Solstice, when a grand procession was formed. The Druid priest, in his white robes, went into the forest in search of the Divine Mistletoe that grew on the Oak, when this was discovered a white sheet was spread beneath the tree. The priest mounting the tree, and with a golden sickle cut off the mystic "Branch," and let it fall into the linen sheet. General rejoicing now began. A young bull was tied and offered a sacrifice to the new born sun.

This was the festival of the Druids, which subsequently was termed Christmastide. This festival had been celebrated thousands of years before the birth of Jesus the Christ.

I would here ask the question; is there at this day any special Psychological power in the Oak? It lies within the limits of my privileges to answer this question in the affirmative. Yes, this is the Psychic cause of Briton's ascendency over the nations of the earth in the past. Britishers! You are not alive to this occult fact. The Oak is that sacred *Talisman*. The Oak is the living *Talisman* which accounts for the superiority of this country. Please note the following: At the time when our Oaks were abundantly scattered over this land, Britain, as a nation, stood alone. Not only as Mistress of the Seas, but Master of the World! Flatter not yourselves with the fabricated chimera that England's wealth makes her greater today than she was centuries ago. Verily as England has increased in money she has decreased in veritable manhood. Why is this so? Answer: her country is despoiled of her Oaks. The father of trees is cut down, and their ancient site has not been replenished with young ones. Since those days when avarice usurped the domain of veneration; when England began to exterminate her spacious Oak forests; from those days date her decline. Think of these remarks as you may; look on them in what light you choose. Call all I have written but a tissue of superstition the facts are there all the same. I find one satisfaction amid our iconoclastic race: in the parks of our old nobility the grand old Oak may yet be seen in his primal greatness. Hence the venerators of the Oak have the blessing of the Oak, for as a *Talisman* its virtues are given to its preservers.

The Healing Power of the Oak

The strengthening influence of what this tree is capable of affording the prostrate invalid is great. The following complaints are among those for which it is specially applicable: prostration after long illness; a sensation of an all-gone feeling; a giving up of all, and everything, great timidity; and a constant dread of death. For each and all of these complaints the Oak is the remedy. The aura of this tree is deep golden. It very much resembles the aura which belongs to the sun; hence the applicability of its primal name, the *fire of the gods!* The solar influence of the Oak transmitted directly to a mortal in the body would be too positive, and would bring to bear on the organic structure more life force than that organism could endure, which implies sudden death to the subject of that influence.

It thus happens that the cause of sudden death is not for lack of life force, but the lack of an instrument capable of holding that force. It is therefore, in most instances, that more attention should be paid to the repairing of deranged or damaged tissues, and the removal of obstructives, than to the augmentation of the life forces. Why is it that sudden death is very often the sequel to a state of excitement? It is — in part at least — when the bodily organism is excited there is extra friction, friction beyond that ordinary friction which nature requires, and, as the ordinary life currents are kept in motion by friction, so that when more than the amount of ordinary friction is produced, a more than ordinary life current is stimulated into activity. Thus the strain becomes too great for the organs to endure and sudden death is the result. But God, in his providence, has so far adjusted natural laws, that those positive forces in nature should pass through a medium before being taken up or imbibed by the human organism, by which arrangement the force is modified and prepared for those purposes in nature as may be required.

The Oak is a medium for a special solar ray, which being mingled with other elemental essences, is capable of imparting to the man who may have the requisite wisdom, new life and renewed vigour. The invocative word belonging to the ritual for the Oak is DUW-ARCHUA, which should be repeated *seven times*, slowly and reverentially, with face to the North.

This is the sigil

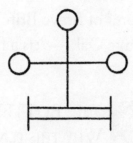

of the Oak.

The word for invocation is

DUW–ARCHUA

THE SONG OF THE OAK

The forests and fountains, the shady Alcove,
Are said to be under the ruling of Jove.
This Lord of the spaces is said to control,
The fire celestial, that realm of the soul!

In the kingdoms of nature, among Jove's decrees
I find it recorded, his favourite of trees
Is the one 'neath which to the Druids, he spoke,
That King of the forest, the Noble Old Oak.

Thou Ashel of Hebrew! thou Druse of the Greeks!
The Derw of Britain! thy power yet speaks;
Through a son,[†] of Brave Briton this caution is given
Spare the brave Oak — 'tis a favourite of heaven.

THE BUTTERCUP (*Ranunculus*)
WHY THIS PLANT SHOULD BE CALLED CROWFOOT IS TO ME A PUZZLE; AS THE NAME RIGHTLY INTERPRETED IS FROG-FOOT, HOWEVER, WHAT IS WRITTEN, IS WRITTEN; AS IT IS BY THIS NAME OF CROWFOOT THIS PLANT IS NOW RECOGNISED. I THEREFORE SUBMIT TO AUTHORISED CUSTOM. THE COMMON MEADOW CROWFOOT FORMS THE SUBJECT OF THIS FIRST CHAPTER IN THE NEW SERIES. IT IS NOT NECESSARY I should give a description of this plant, seeing it is one so familiar to all who may have wandered occasionally through the fragrant pasture lands of this country in the summer months. The children of rural districts are familiar admirers of the Buttercup.

---

† Charubel

As I see this plant in my psychic condition, and from a soul point of view, it has a purple stem and yellow flower. The flower has three rows of *petals*. The centre contains a deep red *Pistil*, broad at the base, but tapers to a point at the top. Such then is the interior beauties of the little Buttercup, beauties are these which never fade!

But it is not necessary all who read these words should see as I see, any more, than that the many thousands of scientific facts should be realised by the multitude, individually, by the tardy process of primal experimentation, in order to derive from this and other plants their occult properties; or otherwise to transmit to others those properties, providing the one you desire to benefit be known to you.

The Crowfoot tribe are all more or less poisonous, they abound with an acrid juice which is dangerous, more especially the BUTTERCUP. This plant has been known to cause dangerous ulcers to develop on the hands, from having handled them too freely, hence, such plants, however fascinating their flower might be, should not be handled too caressingly. On the soul plane the Buttercup is yet even more poisonous. Although with this difference: you cannot on the soul plane give the patient this poison; hence if a person were to desire to injure another with the psychic poison, it would have no other effect than this: it would take from the person an evil, to which it may be in sympathy, and this would disarm the person of a certain virus, by which it would prove a blessing and not a curse. Hence the laws on which all power connected with Psychic Botany, are in direct opposition to the principles and practices of *Black Magic*. Yes, for the connecting a person to a poisonous plant, does not poison the individual thereby, instead you take from that person the poison abounding in his nature to which the poisonous plant may be in sympathy. And further, an evil disposed person cannot take an active part in these operations without receiving a personal good, and by such a practice finally become a better man. Seeing the Buttercup has such properties on the soul plane, what are those evils which this little plant is capable of healing? Those who are addicted to weeping, from no other cause than a consciousness of an undefinable gloom, a species of melancholia, a looking back, a longing for gone by scenes, an old home; departed friends; vanished pictures of hopeful days; anticipations unrealised; suicidal tendencies. There is one other physical evil for which this little plant is a psychopathic remedy: great heat in the face and forehead, and inflamed eyes.

This is the sigil

of the Buttercup.

The word for invocation is

RO—VAM—HAI.

The person in need of the remedy must repeat the word
eight times slowly.

> These truths to me have long been given
> By sages on earth, whose lives are in heaven.
> These teachings of Nature I give here to you
> Is wisdom celestial, received by the few.

THE WILD ANEMONE (*Ranunculae*)
THIS LITTLE PLANT GROWS ON DRY DITCH BANKS NEAR TREES OR WOODED PLACES. IT FREQUENTLY INVADES THE PASTURE LAND WHICH MAY LIE IN PROXIMITY, WITH, OR NEAR ITS ORIGINAL SITUATION. IT IS OF LOW and slender growth, rising not more than from three to six inches above the ground, and bears a white, blue, or purple flower. Its leaves spread near the ground, and where they exist, there no grass can grow, they thus become a pest to the agriculturist. The flowers do not long remain, after the flower is left behind a small tuft of feathery tails, or oval woolly heads in place of the clusters of grains which are found in the Ranunculus. These tails are the *styles* of the *Carpel*, grown large and hairy, and these serve as wings, by which the seed is carried by the wind to distant places, where they alight, germinate, and grow. In this way large tracts of pasture land is rendered unproductive.

The WILD ANEMONE flowers towards the end of April, and the whole of the month of May. The leafy part of this plant, with its stem, is frequently a beautiful purple. The shape of the leaf bears a striking resemblance to the MEADOW CROWFOOT. Not so the flower.

THE PSYCHIC ANEMONE

THE COLOUR AND FORMATION OF THIS PLANT, AS IT APPEARS TO ME ON THE SOUL PLANE, IS THE FOLLOWING: THE ROOT AND LOWER STEM IS BLOOD RED. THE BRANCHES, AS THEY ASCEND, ARE DEEP PURPLE AT FIRST, BUT GRADUALLY THEY DEVELOP INTO BLUE, AND FINALLY, THE LEAVES develop into deep green. The flowers are not open as on the earth plane, but assume a globular shape as if wrapped up in *Perianthine* folds, and that so closely as to be scarcely distinguishable, so that outwardly there appears to be more nor less than a globular protuberance. Plants having such characteristics on the soul plane are capable of numerous transformations and enlargements under the hands of a scientific florist, or horticulturist, on the physical plane. For however much the florist, or gardener, may pride himself on his skill, in the production of varieties from a given species; there are limitations, beyond which no human skill will ever pass. The potentialities of a given species are all treasured up in the psychic germ, and it is only to the degrees of such potencies the artist may change, transform, or enlarge, but no further.

I now come to a more important part of Psychic Botany, that each plant possesses special characteristics, which are allied not only to certain complaints, but to sex, age, and temperament. This phase of the subject has not been previously noticed, simply that the full, or more complete knowledge of these matters had not been attained to. The Wild Anemone, like others of the Crowfoot family, is poisonous; and is negative to the complaints for which it is the cure. This plant is in sympathy with that evil which produces valvular affections of the heart; gouty pains in various parts; hemicrania accompanied with great heat in the left cheek and temples; a flow of hot tears from the left eye; and inflamed kidneys. It is to the female sex this plant applies, and more especially to those of dark complexion, and between the age of twenty-five and forty. It answers the male sex, only in a less degree.

This is the sigil

of the Anemone.

THE CLEMATIS (*Crowfoot Family*)

THIS PLANT IS KNOWN IN THIS COUNTRY BY THE NAMES OF TRAVELLER'S JOY AND VIRGIN'S BOWER. THE LATTER BEING A SPECIES CULTIVATED IN GARDENS. BUT, AS BOTH THE WILD SPECIES AND THE CULTIVATED ONE POSSESS THE SAME PSYCHIC PROPERTIES, I NEED NOT MAKE ANY FURTHER REMARKS ON CHARACTERISTICAL differences which might further be traced, and which after all, would prove but unimportant. Every variety of Clematis are of the genus of climbing plants. There are but few points of resemblance in this plant to the Crowfoot tribe.

The CLEMATIS is, I believe, the only plant of the order of *Ranunculae* having woody stems. It is a plant that will attach its tendrils to any thing, by way of support, and may be trained to any shape you choose. The flowers are deep purple; nor do they bloom till the end of summer, they then exhibit their beauties, when the earlier summer flowers are faded.

This plant is, in appearance, the same on the psychic plane as it is on the physical, from which I conclude it has attained its full state of development. I am therefore inclined to consider the CLEMATIS, either in its wild state, or under cultivation, as not capable of further changes through cultivation. It appears to be the consummation of an order of floral development.

The classifications we have on the outer plane are very superficial. At the same time it is well our Scientific Botanists have done what they have, it has proved of great service to mankind in the different departments of life, more especially in the culinary and medical departments. It is invariably the natural tendencies and habits of plants that determine their classification on the soul plane; much the same as it may be with the soul of a being of a higher organization. I notice in the next place the class of diseases for which the Clematis has a pathological sympathy: An inflamed groin; intense pains in the legs and thighs. Acrid virus in the blood. It is of value in all cases where germinal scrofula may be suspected, as lying dormant in various parts of the system. For, although it be not able to combat scrofula in its more developed forms, it has, under all conditions, the property of nullifying it in its incipient stages. It is better adapted in these complaints in the male sex, than the opposite; and that from the age of 30 to 50, more especially men of bilious temperament; dark, or swarthy complexion, and of square build.

This is the sigil

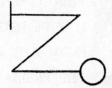

of the Clematis.

The word for invocation is

ZA–RA.

This word should be repeated seven times, in a reverential state of mind. The best time for this ritual is any time between the hour of sunset and midnight. Make the plant negative to the disease — the Scapegoat to carry all away.

THE MONK'S HOOD
(*Crowfoot Tribe*)

THE MONK'S HOOD IS THE MOST POISONOUS OF THE CROWFOOT FAMILY. IT IS SAID TO BE FOUND WILD IN THIS COUNTRY, BUT I DO NOT HOLD THIS TO BE TRUE. FOR, ALTHOUGH IT MAY BE FOUND IN A LOCALITY FAR FROM ANY HUMAN DWELLING, YET, THE PROBABILITY IS THAT IT WAS CARRIED THERE FROM A PLACE WHERE IT EXISTED UNDER CULTIVATION.

The sepals and petals of its flower are purple-coloured. There are five sepals, and one of these is very large and resembles a kind of helmet, which overshadows the other part of the flower; there are only two of the petals fully developed. These are two fleshy bodies mounted on long stalks, projecting into the helmet. Both leaves and roots of this plant are very poisonous, the roots especially so. It flowers in July; and thrives best in damp places. This plant may be found in most flower gardens, and not infrequently its roots are in proximity to those vegetables which are used as edibles. Thus you may have in your gardens one of the most virulent of vegetable poisons over which there may be but little care, or caution exercised.

There is one peculiar characteristic connected with this plant; heat destroys or extracts the poison of the Monk's Hood branches in a very short time. If the branches be cut and exposed to the hot sun for but a few days they become harmless. To administer this plant as a medicine for any known complaint is very unsafe, unless it be on *Homeopathic* lines, or under the surveillance of a professional practitioner. Not so is this the case on the soul plane. Here this plant may safely be applied without any danger of evil consequences. It is this safety, and security, in the *Psychology of Botany* which renders it of so much service, and value, to all who are interested in its application.

Colds and chills are of frequent occurrence in a climate like our own, where we are subject to sudden changes from heat to cold in summer, and from dry to damp at all times and seasons. How often is it the case, that after free perspiration you sit in some cool place, and a chill is the result, yes, a chill, which in many instances proves fatal. Would you consider a safe remedy at hand, at that critical moment, of any value? I give you this remedy freely. This is more to you than what money can purchase. When you feel a chill from any cause whatever, and under any circumstances, think of the Monk's Hood, picture it before your mind's eye, and whilst doing so, repeat the following invocationary word: LU-VAR-MEL, six times, most deliberately and reverentially, then allow the subject to rest for two hours, when you repeat the same a second time. It is rarely necessary you should repeat a third time. The usual symptoms subside, and a warm glow succeeds the chill; afterwards avoid undue exposure.

This is the sigil

of the Monk's Hood.

The word for invocation is

LU–VAR–MEL.

THE PÆONY (*Said to belong to the Crowfoot Tribe*)

THIS IS, POSSIBLY, THE MOST NOBLE AND BEAUTIFUL FLOWER THAT INHABITS THE FLOWER GARDENS OF THIS COUNTRY. OWING TO ITS MOST BRILLIANT COLOURS, FROM DEEP RED TO CRIMSON, AND EVEN TO WHITE. ANOTHER PROPERTY IS THE LARGENESS OF THE FLOWER. THERE IS A WILD SPECIES THAT GROWS IN THIS COUNTRY, ALTHOUGH, AS I AM INFORMED, IN BUT ONE OR TWO PLACES. THE ONE IS THE ROCKY CLEFTS OF STEEP HOLME (ONE OF A PAIR OF ISLANDS IN THE SEVERN) and may be witnessed in those watering places on the coasts of Somerset, and North Devon. But even in this wild state, I question if it has not originally been brought from some cultured spot. It flowers in May and June. Whatever may be the changes as to variety on the physical plane, there is but one Pæony on the soul plane.

This plant appears to me from a soul point of view of a light golden colour of special brilliancy and lustre. A nimbus of glory surrounds the whole plant; it is in fact unique in this respect.

It holds a special sympathy with that organ designated the spleen, and thus proves itself a generator of the life forces.

Those who may be suffering from great weakness, accompanied with a sense of prostration on the least exertion, a kind of sinking, no pain, no sensation of suffering in any one part of the body more than another, but an indescribable weariness prevails over these much to be pitied mortals. Yes, and even medical men have been puzzled, so as in some instances to attribute the whole to fancy on the part of the invalid. Nor is the patient thought to be ill, and he or she has to *die* to prove to all, the medical man, and the ignorant crowd, that the lady or gentleman must have been ill after all. To all these afflicted ones I point to this beautiful plant, think of it, picture it to your mind, but do not pluck the flower or in any wise injure the plant.

This is the sigil of the Pæony.

The word for invocation is

GROMOGEL.

The Invocative Word is to be used at any time during the day or night, six times.

THE CHRISTMAS ROSE
(*Crowfoot Tribe*)

THIS PLANT IS A FOREIGN SPECIES OF THE HELLEBORE. THERE ARE VARIOUS SPECIES OF THE HELLEBORE WHICH ARE INDIGENOUS TO BRITAIN, AND WHICH ARE TO BE MET WITH IN THE FOLLOWING LOCALITIES:– THE GREEN HELLEBORE IS FOUND IN THE WEST OF ENGLAND; LEIGH WOODS, GRESFORD, AND IN Surrey. This species flowers in April and May. Then there is the Feated Hellebore which abounds in Herefordshire. This species thrives in calcareous soil, and is very rare. But the ordinary Christmas Rose is extensively cultivated in the flower gardens of this country. It has a very marked resemblance to the order *Rosasceœ*. It was formerly held in great repute for its medicinal virtues in the cure of mental derangement.

Dr Carpenter in his great work, *The Physiology of Botany*, makes the following remark: "The Black Hellebore of the ancients grew plentifully at Anticyra, a city of Phosis, in Greece. Whence came the proverb applied to any one who acted in an absurd manner, 'Let him sail to Anticyra.' "

The Christmas Rose opens its large white cups at the close of the year, and blossoms profusely till the end of January. The plant may be said to have a very important history, from the fact, that it is alluded to by the ancients as being a very noted plant in their day. But it adorned the waste places of the temperate zone long before the birth of history. It bloomed amid the mountains, and along the plains of the continent of Atlanta, that vast continent, which now lies submerged beneath the troubled waters of the great Atlantic Ocean!

This plant claims its descent, not from the orient; it courts not the smiles of the sunshine, but is bold and brave enough to exhibit its beauties, defiantly, in the face of a January squall.

The Christmas Rose is pregnant with virtues rare, and valuable; the bulk of which are concealed from the men of science at this day, because these virtues are of a magical character, and do not exist in the domains of what is speculative and necessarily superficial. In the first place, the Christmas Rose is a true product of this planet. Indirectly, it stands related to the moon, for as much as the moon is a part of this globe.

This plant can defy the inclement cold of Winter, and at the most barren time of the year — with us — to shine forth in all its glory. During Midwinter on our side of the globe, the sun being so much nearer the earth than in Midsummer, silently, and in a mysterious way, impregnates our earth with forces, which the summer heat subsequently develops. The, higher influences and the more subtle virtues are stronger in the shade than in the sunshine. The night on the outer plane, is the light of day on the soul plane. The Winter in outer nature, is the season of fruit-bearing on the soul plane. Hence you may rely on it as being a fact; that plants which give forth flower and fruit in the open, in Winter, are no ordinary plants, all such are endowed with uncommon virtues, which it is my mission to make known.

Insanity is on the increase in our land, and I suspect the same remark will apply to other of the so called civilised countries of Europe. I consider I am within the limitation of correctness in saying that the direct cause has ever been: undue excitement; combined with an artificial mode of living. A kind of surface life; where all is but glamour: day dreaming. I am here alluding to the life of our towns and cities, where thousands are rushing daily to and fro in quest of fresh excitement. For such as these the Christmas Rose blooms, just at that season of the year when worldlings pleasures are passing away. This beautiful Winter flower gives a living lesson to the thoughtless and profane; it lives and blooms to teach how man should live, a life superior to, and not depending on, the season pleasures of the year. All cases of insanity; or where there may be a tendency towards insanity, through over excitement; worry, and anxiety.

For such this plant is well adapted. Direct your mind to it; it has magical virtues. The Invocative Word for this Divine purpose is AR—U—MA—PHO—BI—EL.

Repeat this Word nine times, daily, for nine days. Please note:– The ritual must be done by proxy, as the insane could not act for itself.

The one selected to discharge this important function should be a calm thoughtful person, not a novice, nor an unbeliever in what is termed the supernatural. The person selected must be a man, as the female — as a rule — is too negative.

This is the sigil

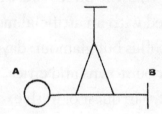

of the Christmas Rose.

The word for invocation is

AR—U-MA—PHO—BI—EL.

This Sigil may be made to any size but the due proportions should be observed. The two sides of the triangle should be of the same length, and the base of the triangle two-thirds of the length of one of the sides of the triangle. The distances from A to the base of the triangle on the left, should be equal to the distance from the base of the triangle to B on the right. Also the same distance as from the apex of the triangle to the crux line, or the tau. I am particular on these matters, for the reason that the Sigil of the Christmas Rose is a *talisman* against excitement, and an antidote for insanity.

It must be engraved on Silver, and carried on your person.

ST JOHN'S WORT (*Hyporicaceae*)

I AM NOW MAKING KNOWN ANOTHER NUMEROUS AND BEAUTIFUL FAMILY OF PLANTS. THREE HUNDRED SPECIES OF WHICH ARE WIDELY SCATTERED OVER THE WORLD; ELEVEN ONLY ARE FOUND WILD IN BRITAIN. THESE MAY BE SEEN ON HEDGE-TOPS IN RURAL DISTRICTS DURING THE SUMMER MONTHS. THE WHOLE OF THE ST JOHN'S WORT ARE HERBACEOUS, OR UNDER SHRUBBY. THE LEAVES ARE SIMPLE AND UNDIVIDED, MOSTLY OVAL, AND USUALLY SET OPPOSITE EACH OTHER.

There are five sepals, two inside and three outside the clayx or cup. The flower is composed of five petals, their sides are often unequal, and sometimes a little gashed. The margin is dotted with black.

The fruit or seed consists of a capsule, berry shaped, which contains an abundance of small seed. There is one peculiarity about the leaves; if held up between the eye and the light they appear full of small holes. That species of the St John's Wort, I am now introducing to the reader, is called the "Common St John's Wort," the same plant may be found on any old hedge-cop, where the soil is never disturbed. It flowers in July; this is the month when this beautiful plant is at its best, and, it is under such circumstances, you are to think of the plant when seeking a benefit from it, the same holds true of any other plant. Suppose your case required that influence given forth by the Oak; you would not think of that tree as it appears in Winter, bereft of its leaves and verdure, you would, on the contrary, think of the Oak as it is when at its best. The same holds true in the case of every plant or tree, including the St John's Wort. Speaking from my own personal experience, my soul has been, on several occasions, strangely and strongly attracted towards this plant. It ever possessed some special charm to me, and that several years before I had taken up systematic Botany as a study.

This special sympathy has influenced me very considerably on the soul plane, and in a less degree on the physical plane.

Note:– You cannot strongly admire an object in nature without being more or less influenced and changed — to some extent — by the object of your love and admiration. This is a subject of much importance, and deserves the particular attention of all. Your love to an animal, if very extravagant, brings you down towards that animal's sphere. But your love for a plant or a tree raises you upward. The soul of a plant or tree has more of the angel in it than what the animal element possesses.

This plant is more especially a psychic remedy; that is, it applies more directly to the soul. It is a soul healer, a soul strengthener, and a soul comforter. There is no one who can think sympathetically of this plant without experiencing strange sensations.

The strangeness of the sensation arises from the fact that a new element enters the domain of the tempest tossed soul; and, whilst there it occupies the place of a new motive force; it acts like a magnet, drawing or attracting the soul forces, thus bracing up the weaker or more feeble propensities, by giving a healthier tone to the whole psychic nature; thus rendering the soul a better medium for the Divine Spirit, by whose promptings the entire person attains to that fixedness of purpose and nobleness of aim, which ultimates in the accomplishment of his Divine mission on this earth.

I find it necessary, whilst speaking of the soul, to express myself clearly once more, relatively to the soul; which is that man is a trinity in unity. The body being the casket of the soul, and the soul is the body of the spirit. The spirit being the Divine Spark which never could have fallen. I now approach symptoms by which you may learn when to appeal to the mystical virtues of the St John's Wort.

(1) A sensation of floating about, no real rest day or night — Insomnia.

(2) Excessive irritability, a temper ever out of joint.

(3) A fear of some unknown trouble about to overtake him.

(4) Suicidal tendencies.

Each and all of these ills have their seat in the soul. The St John's Wort is the Psychic remedy.

This is the sigil

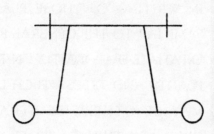

of St John's Wort.

The word for invocation is

THAR–OPHIM.

Note:– Both sides of this Sigil must be of equal length. The top
and bottom horizontals the same length.

THE POPPY TRIBE

I INVARIABLY AFFORDS ME GREATER PLEASURE, IN WRITING OF THOSE PLANTS WHICH ARE FAMILIAR TO THE GENERAL READER, THAN TO EXPATIATE ELABORATELY ON THE PROPERTIES OF PLANTS AND TREES WHICH LIE REMOTE, AND, MAY BE OTHERWISE STRANGERS TO THE ORDINARY THINKER. IT CANNOT BE DENIED, BUT, THAT THE POPPY TRIBE IS WELL-KNOWN TO NEARLY EVERY ONE OF BUT ORDINARY INTELLIGENCE. IN THE MEANTIME, IT IS possible, that the Opium Poppy may not be as familiar as the wild species which may be readily discovered in this land, two species of which I shall duly describe, and the Psychic properties in each instance make known. The first of these is the Celandine — (*Chelidonum Majus*). This little plant grows wild, at the same time it carries the characteristic of a garden outcast. It is of a light green or yellow green foliage. The flowers are deep orange-yellow. When a branch is cut off, a kind of creamy juice oozes out of a pale yellow colour. This plant is most poisonous, and the juice is virulently acrid. There are but few gardens free of this little plant.

Hitherto, the result of my numerous psychical researches has in most instances, been a remedy for some form of internal complaint; but in the present instance I find in the CELANDINE a pleasing variation, in that it presents a perfect remedy for every form of skin-disease, where eruptions of any kind are the leading characteristics. It is but too well-known that such complaints abound to a very large extent, and that these complaints are very annoying to its victim, as well as — in many instances — disfiguring to the general appearance, when the face is the afflicted part. I am convinced, that there are thousands in this country alone, who would give a considerable sum, if by so doing they be assured of a complete eradication of such a pest.

Each reader of this my great work: *"The Psychology of Botany,"* has in his, or in her possession, an easy, safe, and certain remedy, without Pills, Powders, or Lotion. If after this gratuitous revelation and presentation, any one refuses to comply with the conditions, by way of applying so effectual a remedy; then, I must confess, my sympathy for such a one, would be small indeed. There then is your remedy, the CELANDINE you know, you have seen it, it is familiar to you, you who have an ordinary cottage garden, very likely it is there, or may be your neighbour's garden has it. I need not make these homely remarks for the higher classes in society, as they will doubtless have the CELANDINE in their grounds, or otherwise be well informed as to the locality where it may be discovered.

I do not ask you to make a wash for your exanthema, nor yet to run any risk of being poisoned, but to *think* of this plant simply as you would think of an absent friend; you have a picture in your mind of your friend, and the picture is that of the entire person, and not of any particular part of him.

I speak thus plainly as I find within the sphere of my experience, a number of individuals, too indolent to submit themselves to the ordeal of *thinking* even, should such thinking be imposed as a task. I do not allude here to the really afflicted ones, who may find it very difficult to direct their feeble thoughts to any one thing owing to pain, or other long debilitating causes. Any one in true sympathy with the sick, could think for him or her in a formulated prayer, as this may be accomplished by proxy. Then, whilst thinking of the plant, direct your attention from the plant to the complaint. Say to yourself, let this evil go to the plant, I am now thinking of, in that plant it will find a place, and a work for good in the life and growth of that plant, while its absence from this sufferer will leave room for what will bring peace, health, and happiness. At the end of such

musings and thoughtful contemplations, repeat the word MUR–
ROO six times slowly, deliberately, and solemnly.

This is the sigil

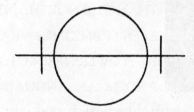

of the Poppy.

The word for invocation is

MUR–ROO.

A perfect circle one inch in diameter. The horizontal passing
through the centre.

CRIMSON CORN POPPY
(Papaver Rhoas)

THIS HAS BEEN FITLY CALLED A "BRILLIANT WEED." IT FREQUENTS WASTE PLACES. MORE ABUNDANT IN THE SOUTHERN COUNTIES OF THIS COUNTRY THAN THE NORTH. NEAR MANCHESTER EVEN IT BECOMES A RATHER RARE PLANT. IT FLOWERS FROM JUNE TO OCTOBER, AND IS AN ANNUAL. THIS BEAUTIFUL plant is a lover of cornfields, which you can easily see at some distance as the deep crimson bloom renders it so conspicuous, and even attractive. It appears to vie with those prouder and much petted beauties of the flower garden. Indeed as an annual there is not one that can surpass it in richness of colour.

The Poppy as a class possesses great tenacity to life; the seed will remain dormant in the ground for years. This is the case when a field that has been long under cultivation is laid down to grass, where the Poppy has abounded and flourished for years; once the field becomes grass the Poppy is seen no longer; at the same time, after a long period of years, when the same field is again under cultivation, the Poppy will again show itself. This has been noticed in deep railway cuttings where the Crimson

Poppy has shown itself the first year. These seeds must have slumbered for ages. I am quite aware that some modern time writers will account for such from other sources than those I have mentioned. Yet I do not see any reason why we should doubt the possibility of a seed, shut out from the light and air, being capable of retaining its vitality for centuries. But to ensure this, the seed must while in its vigour, be in fact hermetically sealed.

There are about 180 species of the Poppy tribe known, two-thirds of which belong to Europe, the remainder are scattered over the globe.

I now come to deal with this beautiful annual psychically and psychomedically. The question which arises here, as elsewhere: For what purpose has this plant been projected on the Physical Plane? For every plant, great and small, has its mission; that mission has been of a far higher order than to please the eye of thousands of superficially minded pleasure seekers, who oft with cruel and ruthless hands will devastate a whole neighbourhood of its lovely floral companions, and that for no other purpose than to hold them, to droop and die, in the hand for a few hours. So much loveliness has not been born simply for you to gaze on. The bloom of every plant and tree is the bridal dress of that plant. The insect tribes in general, and the bee in particular, are fascinated and attracted by those gay colours. It is in fact an invitation to all to come to the floral marriage.

When the little cups are filled with the ambrosial nectar, the pollen is also ready to be taken from the otherwise barren bloom to the fructify one, when the bees and insects are liable to intermix them, owing to the pollen sticking to the insects by the aid of the honey, which must adhere to them. Thus nature pays her little workers for services which they unconsciously render. Seeing such wonders are discoverable on the physical plane, in these strange adaptations and wonderful design; what must be the condition of such plants on the higher planes of floral life? Have we not here proofs of higher and grander designs? Yes, verily, to my knowledge we have. What I tell you in this paper is no guess-work, it is knowledge. I will here give you the result of this knowledge respecting this little plant, the Crimson Cornfield Poppy.

It is a plant on the soul plane; it is a plant in bloom; it appears of the same colour on the soul plane as on the physical. It lives on the soul plane; yes, it lives! But that life is not conditioned as it is now on the earth plane. Its roots do not feed by suction out of the damp, cold earth. It lives by imbibing other essences. It is a living thing, and more than that, it is a semi-intelligent thing. Whilst the plant life is incarcerated in an organised body on earth it often manifests a kind of instinct not far removed from that animal life which may subsequently feed on the plant life. But when it has left its tiny tabernacle on the earth plane, it forms for itself a superior and a more beautiful dwelling, a form which the nipping frosts of winter may not injure, or rude hand destroy. It henceforth lives for the health and happiness of higher intelligences, whom it will serve with its odour as well as its life-sustaining aura.

These plants are all living, semi-intelligent entities, and that man who has advanced to their soul plane, may by sympathy, inhale from those ambrosial fonts health, life, and happiness. It is thus, and in this light I see the present plant bedecked in its gorgeous bridal bloom. Its petals will not fade! It is no longer chained to one poor spot of earth, but freely and majestically floats upon the ether-wave, and may thus become the companion of some solitary soul, who may have looked in vain for sympathy from his fellows.

In these papers I point out the simple way by which the partially developed soul may attract to itself whilst in the body, what may help under sorrow and suffering of various kinds. The animal kingdom are incapable of such virtues from their psychic state.

The complaints for which the Crimson Poppy is adapted, and for which it constitutes a remedy, as follows:–

(1) A deep dull pain in the forehead; more especially at the centre of the forehead, with great heaviness about the eyes and eyelids.

(2) An intolerable want to sleep, but after sleep not refreshed.

(3) Averse to all intellectual labour, living in a kind of stupor state, not unlike the effects from having imbibed a narcotic.

This is the sigil of the Corn Poppy.

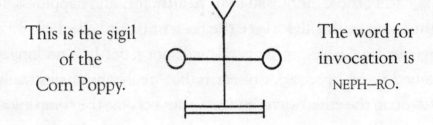

The word for invocation is NEPH–RO.

The word by which you may call, command, or invoke the virtues of this beautiful plant is NEPH-RO This word should be repeated nine times. In the present instance the plant is negative to the disease.

CRANE'S-BILL OR HERB ROBERT
(*The Geranium Family*)

THE CRANE'S-BILL IS A VARIETY OF A RATHER NUMEROUS SPECIES OF THE GERANIUM FAMILY, WHICH ABOUND IN THIS COUNTRY. IT GROWS ON HEDGE BANKS, IN OLD RUINS, ON ROCKS, IN WOODS AND SHADY PLACES, AND IN SOME FEW INSTANCES HAS BEEN FOUND ON THE ROOFS OF OLD THATCHED COTTAGES, AND IN THE CHINKS OF OLD WALLS.

It is, as you may learn from what is here stated, a common plant, as it may be found anywhere.

This plant flowers during the whole of the Summer, and is an annual. The flowers are red, streaked with white; they are small, and the stem proportionately so; the stem is hard, and stands about a foot high.

The one peculiarity about this plant is: the stem is red. It is to this fact we attribute the name Herb Robert, which is a corruption of Rob, or Rub-wort.

This little plant has a lovely appearance, and, seeing it continues in bloom right through the Summer down to dull and chilly November, it may be considered worthy of some attention from us, if only as a rural beauty. But, if you refer to those works which treat of the medical properties of plants, the Crane's-bill is held up and extolled as being a safe and valuable astringent, possessing the power to stop inward bleedings, and of stanching all inordinate fluxes.

I am convinced, that as a physical remedy, a better and safer astringent does not exist, and is good for man and beast.

I will here enumerate some of the more prominent peculiarities by which this plant may be the more readily known. The first is: it has a small star-like flower, red, with small white stripes. Secondly: the stem is red. The third and most characteristical item is: it has a very offensive smell, the smell of a fox.

This little plant is capable of many changes if brought under cultivation. Such possibilities abound on the soul plane; for, as sensed by me on that plane, it appear to assume the dimensions of those under-shrub species of the Geranium family which are the flowerpot beauties of this day, and which form the window ornaments of nearly every cottage in the land.

I am inclined to conclude that the Crane's-bill under proper cultivation might attain to similar proportions, if not to equal beauty. But like changes brought about by cultivation would not affect the nature of this plant on the soul plane.

It is well-known that the physical properties of the medicinal plants are not enhanced, but on the contrary diminished by cultivation. The nearer a plant approaches its native state, the more potent are its medicinal properties. The numerous varieties of the Geranium have all, more or less, those properties in common which have already been alluded to. Such is the case on the soul plane in a more marked degree; and as the Crane's-bill is the stronger, and is characteristically more definite on all those points I am about to mention; I have chosen this plant as being the best type of the Geranium family for those purposes now under notice. I note in the first place the leading characteristics of those Complaints which abound in this country. The greater part of these complaints are, directly or indirectly, attributable to lack of tone. To explain myself more clearly; when there is a certain amount of laxity in the whole of the nervous system, the body becomes open to receive any pernicious germs or miasmata, which may chance to be floating in the atmosphere at the time. It is then and under such circumstances we are most exposed to contagion. To lose tone is to lose vitality, and this cannot take place without a cause.

The cause or causes are; whatever tends towards drawing off from the vitals an inordinate amount of energy. Such as: Worry; intense application of the mental faculties; exposure to cold, and long abstinence from food. Each and all of these tend to draw off the vital force from the body, and that inordinately. Hence all those complaints following such violations of nature's laws will be characterized by lack of tone. For each and all of these, the CRANE'S-BILL is the remedy. It applies more especially to cold natures, and where there may be any tendency towards anaemia, which is common with young women of tender age. To such this plant stands as the remedy.

There is one very painful disease for which this is a cure, and that is Toothache. In most cases this arises from lack of tone, or some want of vitality. The nerves become lax, a virus is generated in the locality of the tooth, which, coming in contact with the diseased nerve, causes irritation and pain. Then there being a special action set up, causing a rush of blood towards the painful part; this is inflammation,

I am using the simple language of a non-professional man; at the same time, it is language capable of expressing the truth. You who may be afflicted with Toothache, more especially if the result of a weak or delicate nature; think of the Crane's-bill.

The word for this plant is ME-VATH-MA. Go over this slowly six times, with your mind fixed as much as possible on the Crane's-bill.

I may here state, that as there is a word for every plant or tree, by the persistent use of which you may command those forces to your assistance; even so is there a sigil belonging to each plant or tree, by the use of which, if rightly applied, the controlling power might be enhanced indefinitely.

This is the sigil of the Crane's-bill.

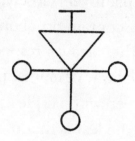

The word for invocation is ME-VATH-MA.

THE COMMON WOOD-SORREL
(*Oxalis-acetosela*)

THERE ARE BUT FEW DRY BANKS BENEATH HIGH SHADY HEDGEROWS DESTITUTE OF THIS SMALL AND FAMILIAR PLANT. THERE ARE BUT FEW CHILDREN IN RURAL DISTRICTS BUT ARE ACQUAINTED WITH THE TASTE OF WOOD-SORREL.

WELL DO I THIS DAY REMEMBER THOSE HAPPY DAYS OF CHILDHOOD, WHEN IN COMPANY WITH CHILDREN OF MY OWN AGE,

I wandered in the woodlands of my native home, in search of what we then called "Cuckoo's-meat." No one, who having tasted the refreshing juice of the Wood-sorrel, could avoid loving it.

The acid is particularly pleasant to the taste. It is said to approach the sensitive plant very closely; as all those plants do, to some extent, which contain an abundance of oxalic acid. They open and shut their leaves responsive to atmospheric conditions, the leaves by way of mutual protection do fold face to face; they are pale green with purple underneath. The bloom is white. The shape of the leaf is that of the Irish Shamrock.

This little plant is capable of effecting much when used physically, and applied outwardly to cancer tumours. I have known handfuls of this plant crushed and folded in wet brown paper, and placed under the hot ashes in one of those grateless fireplaces of the past, by which means the whole was reduced to a pulp, and in that crude state was applied to a large hard lump on the back of the hand as a poultice, and in a short time the whole lump, which was as large as a partridge's egg, was dissolved, and came away, leaving a hole behind, after the manner of a tree that has been grubbed up.

Such is one of the physical properties of this plant. My work, however, is to point out its properties on the soul plane. In the first place, I find this plant of much larger dimensions than what it is on the physical plane. From hence I concluded that it is capable of a higher development on the physical plane.

This conclusion I find, in part, corroborated in a very able work as a text-book, on Botany, by Dr. Grindon. He has the following under Wood-sorrel:– "Half of this family consists of shrubs and trees belonging to the hotter regions of the world." Hence it is as a shrub I see this plant on the soul plane, from which I conclude that the word tree must be an error, that this plant does nowhere assume such proportions as to deserve the name of tree.

In the next place: it appears succulent to a very high degree. Its stem appears like glass with small red stripes resembling the arteries in man. The red hair-like lines appear like those spiral membranes in different stems and leaves on the physical plane, especially that of the Plantain family.

The Wood-sorrel on the soul plane has a very fascinating appearance, which is certainly very suggestive. The next item observable is, that on the soul plane the whole virtue of a plant is to be found in its leaves; "And the leaves of the tree were for the healing of the nations." Again, this plant does not belong to the class of absorbents of evil, but is positive to those conditions for which it might be applicable. The whole of this plant's power and virtues are consummated in the leaves. And why is this the case? On the physical plane all finds its consummation in the fruit. But it must be borne in mind, that on the soul plane seed is no longer requisite. Every plant is henceforth and for ever androgenous! The male and female are united in one, and by virtue of this union there can be no decay. This is the grand climax in the mortal who attains to the immortal state!

The next grand item is:– What are the properties of this plant on the soul plane? It is a life-giver, a vitalizer, an eternal invigorator. It is in fact a tree of life, and it is no wonder that it possesses such attractions to children. Children before being indoctrinated with conventionalism; before being ruined by the so-called education of this day, have some of those native instincts which were implanted in their nature by nature's God. Whilst thus untainted they will spontaneously seek what is natural; hence their love for the Wood-sorrel, by the eating of which they drink into their vital organs of that life-giving stream, and that unconsciously. Every leaf on this small tree of life, like fingers on the human hand, gives out at each small tip that vital force, that will, that power divine, which can raise up and re-invigorate that drooping form, whose fires seem hastening to extinguishment. Think of this plant, O think of this, ye who have long been conversant with your bed, and chamber walls. Your drugs have failed to bring back to you your long lost heritance. Just think of this small plant, entreat its aid by its celestial name AR–VIR–EVEL, and it will glide, like some sweet angel form into your room, and give to you to drink of that ambrosial wine, and raise you up once more to life and happiness.

This is the sigil
of the
Wood-Sorrel.

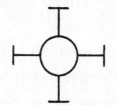

The word
for invocation is
AR–VIR–EVEL.

THE COMMON LIME-TREE
(*Tilia Europœ*)
In describing this tree, I feel there is no necessity for any elaboration on my part, as this tree is so well-known. In the meantime, I will give the reader a fine and poetic description of this tree as given by Dr Carpenter, in his grand work: *Vegetable Physiology*. The following are his remarks:—

"Three species of the Linden or Lime-tree are found in Britain, of which the largest and best known was probably not originally a native of this country.

This last sometimes grows to a great size, and its wood being light, soft, smooth, close grained, and not liable to be worm-eaten, is valued by carvers for ornamental works, and also forms one of the best kind of charcoal for the manufacture of gunpowder.

Its flowers are very fragrant, and are a favourable resort of bees, who obtain from them not only honey but a large supply of pollen, which they store up for the nourishment of their young; and if a hive of bees is at no great distance from a grove of Limes, it may be known when these are in flower, by the large number of bees that will return laden with little pellets of the bright yellow pollen which these blossoms furnish. There are perhaps no trees that form so beautiful an avenue, the peculiar mode in which the branches arise from the stems and meet above, giving them very much the aspect of the Gothic Columns and Arches of a Cathedral; and when the lover of nature walks beneath their luxuriant foliage, "at dewy eve distilling odours," he feels them to constitute a fit temple for the worship of nature's God."

Without further taking up the time of the reader, I proceed to delineate what I see, and will faithfully indite what I may find, by virtue of those senses of my soul, the mystic virtues of the Linden tree upon the psychic plane, whose bows are ample, and whose trunk is large; much larger than any I have seen on the physical plane. The whole of this tree is yellow, a beautiful yellow from stem to branch.

In the meantime there seems to be a fringe of pink at the extremity of each branch, twig, and leaf.

The tree as a whole resembles a distillery, by which a kind of nectar is evolved, which oozes out at every pore, and hangs like crystal dew-drops at the tips of each leaf and petal; these drops keep falling on the place beneath; no drop of this is lost, the whole are gathered up and husbanded with care, by another law of that greater and higher nature which I seek to disclose to you.

Yes, every drop discharged from this psychic tree is collected, and carefully housed within celestial crypts, for the use and nutriment of those whose life no longer feeds on "bread alone."

My soul perceives a hallowed mystery about this tree, which renders it unique. Nature on this outer plane of life — the plane on which we live, move, and have our being — husbands all, no particle is lost.

The vegetation which grows on this surface, when all has perished from our outer gaze, has found its goal. The earth on which it grew and from which, in part, it derived support for a time, receives again its portion of that super-structure. The air, and those more subtle elements: the various gasses, these each receive their own, without a particle of loss or waste. Thus death within the vegetable realm is but the just administer of those accrescent parts, which had been combined in one organic whole, and that to serve a purpose, a purpose but partially understood as yet.

But there is a higher nature, as there is a higher man; and that higher nature has her just claims, claims her own. This higher nature contains the prototypes of all. The so called ideal plant or tree is the real plant or tree, and as the shadow is dependent on the substance for its ephemeral existence, even so, and after the same manner, does this lower nature depend upon a higher. It is thus my higher nature takes note of that sphere where live and bloom for ever, the prototype of plants and trees. It is here I see the Lime-tree.

I now approach the door, which opens at my call, and which conducts me toward a long yearned-for realization! The question I ask is this: Is there but one kind of means by which to prolong life on this earth, within the present body? Must all support of every kind pass through the ordinary process of mastication and digestion? It has been already shown, that to cure those various ills to which humanity are prone, it is not necessary that we should have resort to drugs and potions, taken by the mouth into the stomach. It has been already proved, since my first article on the *Psychology of Botany* appeared, that sicknesses may be cured by a look, accompanied by a thought directed towards a certain plant or tree, without the intervention of other means.

Such has been verified, and that by virtue of our higher nature coming in contact with that higher nature already alluded to, the lower nature may be cured. Do not such thoughts as these open the way, the true and living way, by which this outer nature may be preserved for any length of time? Most assuredly they do.

But here lie those obstacles, which, like those beings with wands of flame, who are said to guard the portal leading to the tree of life, are hard to surmount. There are accidents to which we are daily and hourly exposed. These consist of illness arising from exposure to those inclemencies which prevail in this our clime; arising chiefly from those accompaniments of artificial life, which are those leading characteristics of the present civilization, with which the present race is drenched to saturation.

We have our thousands of manufactories; each of which belches forth its portion of poisonous fumes.

We have our large and thickly populated cities, each containing its background of slums, where live and die unseen, and unlamented teeming thousands, whose dwellings are dens of crime, and where reek those pollutions from whence do rise the "pestilence that walketh in darkness." These poisons permeate the purest atmosphere, nor is there any place out of their reach. Thus we are besieged by foes on every hand, besetting us at every turn through every lane of life. Under such conditions we find it very hard to counteract so many ills. I need not allude to those mechanical injuries to which this organism is open, and by which the present life might be cut off, or otherwise shortened, which at the time may have appeared of too trifling a nature to demand notice.

Then there are those numerous ills with which our nature may be tainted; those dire consequences of what our forefathers may have done, these all combined constitute a formidable army to fight and conquer in this our upward clambering toward the tree of life!

But there is yet another difficulty to contend with: that innate aversion, which abounds in the nature of the present race to all that may pertain to the psychic plane, of things unseen by mortal eyes, whilst at the same time manifesting an idolatrous devotion to the sensuous. Then there is that prejudice, arising from those teachings we have been indoctrinated with from our earliest days, by teachers, preachers, priests and parsons; that to die is the will of God.

In support of these we have those thousands of weeklies, monthlies, and quarterlies flowing from the press, the keynote of which is: "that it is appointed unto men once to die"; all preach death simply because the way to death is easier than it is to climb the steep and rugged path that leads to life.

I teach the way to life, and that at the risk of being called an Enthusiast, which I have been called by a latter-day-light. But such has been the fate of all who have dared to cut themselves adrift from that commonplace claptrap which is in vogue among the smart writers — so called — whose chief mission appears to be to laugh down the truth under every guise.

The false is the fashionable, and therefore the most popular among the currencies of this day. I tell you in my little sheet a truth which you may treat as you choose; this truth is: that the Lime-tree does yield a food on which the enlightened soul may feed, by virtue of which this body may imbibe a sustenance or support, so that when this outer nature is deprived of its wonted supply of grosser food, the adept may have a food to eat which the world knows not of. I do not mean to convey the idea that the Lime-tree is the only tree within the spacious garden of my God; no, there are others, most of which remain to be made known in future papers. But for the present, allow me to direct you to the Lime-tree. Thus to prove the truth or falsehood of what I state, you have the opportunity of testing.

There are complaints whose chief or only symptom is weakness; a gradual sinking; the food taken into the stomach seems to do no good, yields no support.

The afflicted one weakens day by day, with no pain in any part; yet no one appears to understand or to diagnose the cause. Such cases do frequently abound, and all that the Profession seem able to say, is, that such are recognised, generally, under the designation of "General Debility." My friend! The seat of such lies in the soul; the soul is sick indeed and of a truth, nor is there any remedy upon this outer plane of life save in the psychic aura of the Lime-tree.

The Lime-tree yields that food which can supply the sinking soul with what it needs; so that by virtue of the same the outer body will begin to thrive, and shortly will regain its normal strength; and the flush of youthful vigour will return.

Thus the Lime-tree is the specific remedy for that depletion and want of vigour, which may be the result of lingering illness of any kind.

I have given sufficient information in the present paper to enable the man or woman, who can think, to grasp one of the grandest truths of this or any other age! A way is opened up by which the life of this body may be prolonged on this earth, and that indefinitely.

This is the sigil of the Lime-tree.

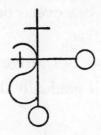

The word for invocation

is TRI—VOO.

You may invoke the mystic virtues of this wondrous tree, to raise you from a bed of sickness to a state of health; or to prolong a life of usefulness on this earth.

133

THE MALLOW FAMILY
(*Althœ'a Officinalis*)

I NEED NOT EXPATIATE ON THE NUMEROUS VARIETIES OF THIS PLANT WHICH ABOUND; ON A ROUGH CALCULATION THEY ARE ESTIMATED AT 1000. BUT THE HOMES OF A GREATER PART OF THESE ARE SAID TO BE THE TROPICS, WHERE THE MALLOW ASSUMES THE DIGNITY OF A shrub or tree. I shall, however, confine myself to but one of these:– THE MARSH MALLOW.

This little plant does not thrive very well in the Northern Counties of England. It gradually dwindles in size the further North it appears.

My authorities say its localities are Salt-marshes, the Banks of Tidal Rivers, the South of England and Ireland. But I can find it plentifully distributed in places where there are no Salt-marshes, or Tidal Rivers. I have found the Common Marsh Mallow growing luxuriantly on the highway-sides in my native county, Montgomeryshire.

This plant grows from two to three feet high, is branched and velvety in every part. The leaves are undivided, or three-

134

lobed; flowers; pale rose-colour, almost sessile in the axils of the upper leaves, or disposed in leafless spikes.

This plant is so well-known to country people generally, I need not waste time and occupy space with superfluous descriptions. Please note: the Cotton Plant belongs to this same family; likewise the showy Hollyhocks now naturalised in our gardens.

The one characteristic of the Mallow is its yield of mucilage; which is a well-known remedy for pectoral complaints such as old coughs, more especially if accompanied with soreness.

Country people are in the habit of making strong decoctions of this plant, mixed with honey, for these complaints, with good result.

There is one item of value to state with respect to the Mallow family, which is: there is not a poisonous species among them, hence they are destitute of any active properties when applied in the ordinary way. But I hope I may be able to show you that the Mallow family in general, and the Marsh Mallow in particular, have active properties when applied as directed in these papers.

I have already explained the whole process of healing by this means, that no more need be said on these lines.

I shall now proceed to notice those forms of disease for which the Marsh Mallow is the antidote.

Hay-fever, extraordinary discharge from the nose with frequent sneezing, attended with restlessness. It would cure Influenza if applied in time.

This is the sigil of the

Marsh Mallow.

The word for invocation is

APH—HI—MOO.

Should you, after all I have written, not know this plant; I feel certain that you would derive benefit by the use of this simple Invocation. The same holds true with the other plants.

THE ORANGE TRIBE
(*Aurantiacœ*)

I FEEL I COULD NOT DO BETTER IN DESCRIBING THIS PLANT THAN TO GIVE MY READERS A QUOTATION FROM MY FAVOURITE AUTHOR, DR. CARPENTER, IN HIS *VEGETABLE PHYSIOLOGY*.

"THE GROUP OF PLANTS PRODUCING ORANGES, LEMONS, LIMES, AND THE LIKE, IS READILY distinguished from the rest of the Vegetable kingdom by several evident characters, which give to its structure much interest; and it is also one of great value to Man, on account of the large quantity of grateful and refreshing fruit with which it supplies him, in the very climates where it is most needed. It is remarkable as being the only tropical fruit which can be introduced into this country, at a cost little exceeding that of our ordinary native fruits; and whilst it thus offers a gratification within reach of the poorer classes, it is so superior to other fruits that it cannot be despised for its cheapness even by the richest. It has been calculated that an average of nearly a dozen Oranges to each individual are annually imported. This abundance is due in part to the prolificness of the tree. It is also due to certain qualities in the fruit itself, which allow it to be kept for a considerable time with less alteration than fruit of any other kind.

If we examine any plant of the Orange tribe, grown in a hot-house in this country, or in the open air of its native clime, we may at once observe that it has a peculiar aspect, in consequence of the surface of its leaves being covered with minute yellowish dots. These dots are little receptacles for secretion, filled with an essential oil very fragrant to the smell, though acrid to the taste; the leaves possess some fragrance in their natural state, but if they be crushed between the fingers this is very much increased, part of the receptacles being then ruptured. These little cavities exist not only beneath the surface of the leaves and fruit, but also in the leafy parts of the flower, which owes much of its fragrance to them. The petals in the Orange are fleshy and white, with dots of green."

Having given the above lucid and interesting description, it will be my mission to make known the healing, and the otherwise wonderful virtues of this tree on the psychic plane. It is a well-known truth that the Orange plant, consisting of the tree, flower, and fruit, possesses a strange fascination for every one.

Hence the Orange Blossoms are the favourite ornaments in the head-dress of those bridal decorations, which it is the privilege of the wealthy to make use of, and so highly are such ornaments prized, that where the genuine blossoms are unprocurable, the artificial ones are substituted. I know, that where so much partiality is shown towards a certain plant or flower, that it proceeds from a higher source than caprice, or of modern conventionalism. Nor does such owe its existence to some accidental exploit on the part of the devotees of fashion. Nor is it the off-spring of reason, nor yet of all the functions of the brain combined. But it has its origin in the ideal; and, although man might not be able to realize that ideal whilst here "in the body pent," were it not that he possesses an organism, which enables him to make known on the outer plane of life; in the meantime this organism is not the creator of that ideal; and as I have elsewhere remarked, the ideal is the real. The ideal exists on the soul plane.

The Orange Blossom with its parent tree existed anterior to the birth of history; and, not only is this the case with reference to its psychic state, but it did so in materialized form, at a period long before that Eden mentioned in our Bible, where our first parents were supposed to be occupied amid the fruits and flowers of a prolific garden, abounding in trees of every kind, the Orange tree being one. This Edenic state which the sacred historian has furnished in mythic garb adorned, is but the reflection of a time long anterior to that; an age which preceded a mighty cosmic change, when man as man did live on such delicious fruits as only God could give.

In the far past I look, where I descry an age sublime; an age that far transcends all those conceptions which we now possess. In fact, the whole as it is seen by me, is so unlike the present state of things, that it is no easy matter to find such words as are capable of conveying correct ideas to my readers; and as to comparisons:–

All such are modern pictures, and must be each confined
To antiquated notions respecting human kind.
Unlike are all of these, to those by poets given,
To what they term the beautiful,—their pictures bright of heaven.
That human race was human, their life the life of soul,
They had no evil passions to kill, or to control.
That Race did not then propagate, as since they've done on earth;
The animal conceptions were not the source of birth.
Each one found its own partner, as birds their mates do find,
Save this, — the animal was absent 'twas mind joined to mind,
They had their Celebrations, when each in love did meet,
Their one Celestial Symbol: The Orange Blossom sweet.

This was to them the Symbol of mystic progeny,

A birth, — most strange development! not "Old mortality!"

By virtue of this union, which was the two in one,

The negative was Luna, the positive, the Sun.

The Race was thus developed, in that grand age of old,

Which Prophets since have dreamed of; that lustrous Age of Gold!

The wisdom I impart to thee, is from an Ancient Sage,

One who lived when time was young: lived through that golden age.

Death had not begun its reign, the earth was not man's doom;

But human life was "evergreen," its happiness the bloom

Of that strange plant, so much esteem'd; throughout the world 'tis
    known;

The Orange it is called by you: its seed preserved — was sown

By angel hands, who yet do live, as we do ne'er grow old;

The Orange tree has been our care e'er since the age of gold.

One favour I do ask of thee, which if thou dolt concede:

Just write what I now give to thee that all who choose may read.

Seek not to make one sentence short, another sentence long,

For what I give is more to thee than manufactured song.

The Orange tree developed so a virtue rare and pure,

It answered well in days gone by; it was the only cure

For discords on the psychic plane, some friction, or some jar;

When happiness was out of joint, and there was psychic war.

'Twas at such times the Orange Bloom was sought throughout the land;

And then when found, all stood around, a circle hand in hand.

This famous tree stood in the midst, each one did on it gaze,

Whilst from the petal of each flower there issued a blaze.

Such flames were frequent in those days; the soul did this absorb,

All eyes could see such lights as these, for then the human orb

Was one, — the soul within — all nature like a glass

Was mirrored in the inner man, and nothing then could pass

Unnoticed by the watchful eye, each one was then a Seer;

For in that mirror of the soul, God's secrets all were clear.

The Orange Bloom, so pure, so white, and free from any stain,

Did symbolize in days gone by, a birth without that pain;

A pain which since has been the lot of every mortal dame.

No state on earth is now exempt, for high and low the same,

Must pass that dire ordeal through, because of that sad fall,

When psychic man became the beast, he since has been in thrall.

The brutish life had charms for him, its loves he did admire,

And thus to find an earthly gem, he waded in the mire.

But must he evermore be thus, and may he not return?

Is that celestial lamp of Life which once on earth did burn,

Extinguished for evermore in one eternal night?

No son of man, I say to thee, I see a prospect bright.

There are a few amid the wreck, as in those days of old,

Who shall attain to Paradise, another age of Gold.

But I must now proceed to tell more of the Orange tree,

What virtues it doth now possess, for this sad century.

And though but few will heed my words, when I have said the whole;

Yet, I will make this matter plain, 'tis healing for the soul.

When sorrow hangs upon the mind, and bitter grief within,

No comfort can'st thou find on earth, thy prospects all are dim.

When melancholy like a pall, prevents the light of heaven

From entering thy troubled mind: when from the strand thou'rt riven.

Direct thy thoughts to this old tree, gaze on its lovely bloom;

Just think of those, the Sons of Light, who triumphed o'er the tomb.

Direct thy thoughts to One Supreme, who lives in all you see,

Then thou wilt find a virtue flow, right from the Orange tree.

This is the sigil

of the Orange Tree.

THE FIR TREE (*Coniferea*)

IT IS NOT MY INTENTION TO WASTE TIME AND OCCUPY SPACE WITH DESCRIBING THIS TREE, AS IT IS WELL-KNOWN TO ALL. BUT I SHALL DEVOTE SOME SPACE IN ORDER TO GIVE TO THE READER SOME OF THOSE CHARACTERISTICS WHICH ARE PECULIAR TO THE FIR FAMILY. FIRST: THIS TREE MAY BE CALLED A CITIZEN OF THE WORLD, AS THERE ARE BUT FEW COUNTRIES WHERE THE FIR TREE DOES NOT GROW. SECONDLY: THOSE LOCALITIES WHERE MANUFACTORIES ARE ABUNDANT; AND WHERE SMOKE AND POISONOUS FUMES DO PERMEATE the atmosphere, there the Fir tree will not grow. Hence it is that Lancashire is nearly destitute of the Fir tree, or it cannot be found in any abundance. I have known gentlemen who have tried to get the Fir tree to grow among other trees about their dwellings but have always failed. It is true that the nature of the soil may have something to do with this absence of the Fir in Lancashire; as this tree will not grow very well in ground that possesses much lime in its composition; and as clay and marl which constitute the greater part of Lancashire contains much lime, this may, in a measure, account for that lack of the Fir we note generally in the said county. The Fir flourishes best of all in the old red sandstone. There is a quality of bog where the Fir will not refuse to grow. As a rule, you will find it partial to dry ground, and waving its sombre branches in the pure mountain air. In the next place I note the antiquity of the Fir family. To trace its noble pedigree it is useless to turn to human records as all these are but as yesterday. I would have you turn over those geological strata, and carefully inspect those coal formations, and you will discover, perhaps for the first time, that what you are burning is, in the main, but the remains of what constituted dense forests of Fir or Pine, which lived luxuriantly, decayed and died during thousands, yes, tens of thousands of years ago, and finally became entombed through a geological break-up, and in this way, its oils and gasses have been preserved for an unborn future. Nature loses nothing, all fragments are carefully husbanded by her frugal hand.

I shall in the next place notice the form, or shape of the Fir tree. There is one letter of the Hebrew Alphabet named Shin, which in its present form resembles the trident. This was not its shape originally. Its original form was that of a pointed cross, which was but a copy taken from the Fir tree, or, more correctly, the Fire tree.

How came this tree to have this name? I will try to explain this matter: You may be aware that the Fir family are cone bearers, cones are pyramidal, that is a form resembling a flame ascending upward; hence the prefix "pyr" also the word "pure" which is the Greek for fire. Again we find "pher" in the Hebrew signifies the same thing. In the name of the wood called Gopher wood of which the Ark was made, we have "pher" as a root wood which points to the fact that the Ark was made of a species of the Fir family. If you note well the arrangement of the branches of the Fir tree, you will perceive they are cruciform; each branch set opposite each other attached to its parent stem, thus forming the upright and horizontal! Thus what we, in this age, call the Fir tree, or Fire tree; the race of the golden age called the life tree or tree of life. This tree being cruciform is a living symbol of the ideal tree of life! The cross and the cone being true emblems of the hidden fire of the gods. I shall close these remarks with some interesting reflections taken from that very comprehensive work "British and Garden Botany," by Dr Leo H. Grindon.

"Whatever be the reason, or which ever way we turn in the Pine woods, we are impressed more than anywhere else in living nature with the idea of unchangeableness; according to our mood it seems a place from which life has passed away, or which is not subject to life and death — in either case the influence is a subduing one, though in a little while like that of the sea it brings enthusiasm and noble thoughts. The more so from the sound of the wind among the tops, which is not that of the ordinary broad-leafed forest, but one peculiar to the Pine wood. More than that of any other trees the murmuring of the Pines carries us away to the shores of the sea, seeming not so much their own as a far reaching and immortal echo. No wonder that those who have lived much near the sea or who have been accustomed to muse upon unfrequented shores with little other company than that of their own souls, going thither, not like Achilles for assuagement of wrath, but for new life, — no wonder that to such the "music of the Pines" is as ones language heard unexpectedly in a foreign land. Other trees in a thousand kinds are evergreen, yet none are evergreen as these are. Only in Spring and in early Summer, at the time of flowing of their annual tide of life is the colour relived, then only at the extremities of the branches where the growth appears either as a light and grassy tuft, or shoots out into a beautiful two-fold spray, flat and horizontally, as a swimmer stretches his hands for the onward stroke. In Autumn the sombre foliage contrasts with the gay hues of the Maples, not as that of Laurels and Hollies, but after the manner of ancient temples that check our views of a tinted sunset; later again, in the deep hush of the snow when most other trees are converted into white miracles of frost and crystal, the Pines still maintain their dark indifference, or if partially overpowered they remind us in the distance of the ermine of the Alps, where branches are represented by whole forests."

The Psychic virtues of the Fir Tree

I am convinced that there is no forest tree which holds so important a place as the Fir tree as seen by me from a Psychic point of view. This tree being of a very positive nature is a giver and not a receiver. It follows, that the spacious Pine forests of this globe are constantly giving from their countless branches an influence as well as aroma, the nature of which is a disinfectant or atmospheric vitalizer, it is in fact the grand healer of the nations; as those abundant emanations, issuing forth from the Pine forests of the globe do permeate the atmosphere, and are wafted by ariel currents through those Azoic dens, where poverty stows away its numerous victims within those hidden recesses, where filth and crime abound.

The planting of the Fir or the Pine should be promoted if only for ordinary sanitary purposes. But this wonderful tree in its Psychic condition surpasses my highest conceptions of beauty and of colour, with perfection in point of organic and divinely artistic proportions, presenting to my vision an equilateral triangle, mounted on an upright stem. The branches arranged, and apparently giving out, from celestial needle-shaped leaves, colours of variegated hues.

At the apex of the triangle, I perceive a radiance, in shape resembling a sunflower, whose centre is brown and whose petals are golden. All the other parts abound in a halo of colours, scintillating in all the glory of the rainbow fringe! Of such as this are the trees and foliage which constitute the sylvian bowers of the "Summer land."

What I am here picturing are not mere reflections reflected from the Fir or the Pine forests of this world. They are but feeble attempts on my part to describe a portion of the immortal Botany of the heavens. The Spiritual and the Psychical are the substance, what we see with mortal eyes are shadows.

Its Healing Virtues

The complaints to which the Fir tree applies pathologically are of the following style:– General languor or an oppressive feeling of exhaustion; a sallow complexion arising from a sluggish liver; a weak and intermittent pulse, and a feeling of faintness. These are a few of the leading symptoms for which the Fir tree provides an antidote. To obtain benefit, or a cure, it is not necessary that the patient should be clairvoyant so as to see this tree psychically, or yet even to think of it psychically, but simply hold it in your thought as a thought picture. This method

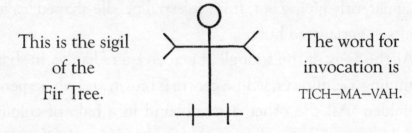

This is the sigil of the Fir Tree.

The word for invocation is TICH–MA–VAH.

of healing may be effected by proxy; another may think for the patient; this may be done at any distance from the patient, and that without his or her knowledge. All I here affirm may be accepted as true, as what I here state is neither more nor less than what I have repeatedly tested.

The Invocation

There is not a force in nature but may be excited or enforced to act on certain lines, and that for a certain determinate purpose as the active agent might select. To aid such active and intelligent agents there are instruments specially adapted for to awaken such forces as may belong to a particular plant or tree. The word for the Fir tree is TICH–MA–VAH. The first syllable is a guttural, the ch requiring the lower part of the tongue to express it forcibly.

THE YEW TREE.

THE PRESENT PAPER IS DEVOTED TO THAT WELL-KNOWN SPECIES OF YEW, WHICH ABOUNDS IN THE OLD GRAVEYARDS OF THIS COUNTRY. ALL OF A DESCRIPTIVE NATURE WILL BE DISPENSED WITH, AS THIS SPECIES — THE OLD ENGLISH YEW — IS FAMILIAR TO ALL. I SHALL, IN THE PRESENT INSTANCE, DEVOTE SOME SPACE TO THE HISTORY OF THE OLD ENGLISH YEW. IN THIS DEPARTMENT OF MY PRESENT ARTICLE I AM OBLIGED TO TURN ON MY OWN RESOURCES; SUCH AS I POSSESS within the domain of soul, as on the outer plane, so far as authorities are concerned all is blank.

The pedigree of this tree, as well as that of its numerous allies, is a parallel with the Fir tree, to which it bears a rather striking resemblance; but which is, after all, of a different order. The Yew is an order of plant life that partakes of both the Fern and the Fir. It may be said to form a connecting link between these two. In the order of cosmic development the Yew stands anterior to the Fir or the Pine. The Yew adapts itself to any country, and that without but very few changes in its structural appearance.

The Yew grows to a large tree in China. In Japan its leaves resemble the foliage of the Maiden-hair Fern; in the meantime it is with our grand old English Yew that I am now concerned.

This tree grew in Britain ever since it was an island. It may be truly said to be indigenous to this island, and grew here when no other save the Fern tree abounded. Thus the Yew was the first of flowering and fruit bearing plants then on this island.

It thus stood forth as an index-finger pointing to a new state of development, whilst its leaves point, to some extent, to a dead past, its fruit points towards a better and more hopeful future.

Whilst the leaves of this tree are poisonous, the fruit is luscious, and are eaten by birds and children.

This tree absorbs and dispenses. It absorbs the death principles of its surroundings, and gives out the life principle. Thus you may perceive, in what I say of this tree, that its being the connecting link between the Fern and the Fir, it is rational to suppose the one nature should absorb the evil, and the other should give out the good.

The Ancients, in the far past, looked on this tree as being the Symbol of the planet Saturn and the Sun. Saturn stands for all things mortal, or the termination of the earthy. The Sun, the beginning of a life that shall not be subject to decay and death. Thus the English Yew as it stands at this day in our old graveyards; more especially the old churchyards of Wales, where it abounds to a greater extent than in England; is a very proper Symbol for the mortal and the immortal; death and life; it has been planted by pious hands in our rural village graveyards, as a fit and proper symbol of life and immortality which came to light by the Gospel; and has been made use of in the past ages as the emblem of the Messiah, who took on Himself that nature which had become the subject of death, and in the meantime, by those higher powers of life which He possessed, developed the immortal.

Thus out of death came life, as it was out of darkness that light came. There is a very pleasing disparity between the beautiful pink berries of the Yew tree and its sombre evergreen and poisonous leaves. There is a much more pleasing disparity between the mortal and the immortal in man. The mortal descends, but the immortal ascends.

No one can tell the age of some Yews which I have seen in some of those little out of the way churchyards among the mountains of Wales. I counted seven in a small churchyard among the hills in Denbighshire. But these grand old trees abound and occupy large spaces in most country churchyards; they give a very picturesque aspect to rural villages, which I consider calculated to produce a very pleasing effect on the soul of the thoughtful.

The Psychic Virtues of the Yew Tree

On the psychic plane this tree appears in a different costume. The dark-green foliage is transformed into golden, mingled with azure. From every branch I see a small hair-like stream descending of what looks like Crystalline Nectar. About this tree I see an innumerable host of fairy-like beings, resembling a species of diminutive humanity. Each of these tiny beings are drinking at these crystal currents.

These beings appear to be specially allied to the Yew tree. They are not only feeders on this tree themselves, but they can be made the distributors of its virtues to those whose soul may have an affinity to the sphere of the Yew.

I do feel grateful to heaven for so glorious a revelation; and although but few of my readers will be sufficiently interested in this revelation so as to become the recipients of these mystic virtues, yet I, for one, shall be benefited; seeing I make known to all what I receive, if others are not benefited it will not be my fault.

This tree is not specially for any one form of disease, or such as are recognised as disease. It has more to do with the soul of the individual. Its virtues are expressly to build up the soul, which is the spiritual body. You may have read those words uttered by King David in one of his Psalms: "O spare me that I may recover strength before I go hence and be no more." It is evident that the Psalmist needed his soul strengthened. He must have had, for the time, a glimpse of another and interior body, which needed some little repairs before pulling down the old house. There was an epoch in the far past when man lived more on the psychic than on the so called intellectual plane; this is more than what the present humanity is capable of realising. Our present conceptions of beauty are not in unison with those possessed by man during one of those buried Æons of the past.

Nature closes each door after the birth of her offspring. Thus when one race has completed its round, fulfilled its mission, the door of that degree attained to by that race is closed behind it. The succeeding humanity cannot form any idea as to what may be the conceptions of its predecessor, but the predecessor may form correct notions of its successor. In the meantime, as there are always exceptions to every rule, or in other words, there ever have been those who have lived, whilst members of the succeeding race, the life of its predecessor, and have been able to realise what may have been the leading ideas of that race. But, when these exceptional characters seek to make these same ideas known to their contemporaries they are sure to be misunderstood, and what they say or write, for the time, will not be appreciated.

This tree was known to the Psychic race, who were able to imbibe from its branches, as it appeared to them in that life and on that plane of existence, a support which the humanity of this heady race have no conceptions of. Clairvoyance approaches that life condition; at the same time, neither Clairvoyance, Clairaudience, or Psychometry are to be considered as being identical with that state. It is vain consulting an ordinary disembodied spirit as to the nature of this Psychic race, much more useless to consult modern scientists. There is a phase of untutored and unspoiled childhood, which bears a more striking resemblance to psychic man than any other outward embodiment that I am acquainted with. Hence the applicability of those words of Jesus: "Except ye become as a little child, ye cannot see the kingdom of heaven." That child to whom the Master alluded was not the spoiled, sharp, or precocious child of this nineteenth century, which I designate the heady race, being the antithesis of the soul race.

What I write is but a fragment of the experience of that every day life I am living on the soul plane. The psychic side of nature with her boundless resources are as familiar to me as the hills and valleys of my native land. I come in contact with more there than can be found here; hence the Yew appears more marvellous to me than it does to you. I am not at all surprised, that the good old men of the past should have made choice of this tree as Monarch of the graveyard, and companion of the dead! I hope I may never see the day when this heady race will have attained that degree of turpitude as to cut down this Grand Old Relique of a long lost past; and Survivor of the Cosmic wreck. The noble Oak has been partially destroyed; and as a result the present race are weakened on the outer plane. Should any one presumptuously in my presence take up the axe to fell the Yew I will cry out, not sing out, "Woodman spare that tree, touch not a single bough." In it a past eternity unites the present now.

Who among my readers are capable of being benefited by the psychic nature of the Yew? Those who are highly sympathetic; those who are impressionable; those whose minds are not absorbed in the things of the senses, those who are fond of solitude; those who delight in the contemplation of nature where it is most natural; not the most accomplished; not the most highly educated; nor yet the greatest intellect. As a rule, it may be calculated that the more ordinary samples of humanity are suitable for the reception of those influences and virtues which this wonderful tree possesses.

It has been already stated that the Yew tree is a soul strengthener; but this phrase is scarcely sufficiently comprehensive; I will further say, it includes lowness of spirits, or a sense of great depression, and that when there is nothing in the circumstances of the individual to constitute a real cause for such a state. All such symptoms indicate a weak or infirm soul; and when manifested through the brain, or the outer consciousness is insanity. For this kind of disorder there is no radical cure to be found among the Therapeutics of Medical Science. Nor are there but few of the Profession so bold as to pretend that such may be cured by drugs. Instead of medicine they generally advise change of scenery, cheerful company, or a sea voyage. In the meantime there must be a remedy, but that remedy must be of such a nature as to be capable of reaching the afflicted part, or primary seat of such an affliction. I have, in the Yew, discovered a remedy, one that will absorb that morbific effluvia, which, like the horrid nightmare, clings to the helpless soul — the spiritual body — and at the same time imparts to those psychic wounds a healing balm. Connected with cure are rules and observances to be complied with, as well as an Invocation to be uttered, the whole should be strictly and religiously observed. The best time to apply to the Yew for help is the Seventh hour past noon. The patient or his helper should devote the greater part of the hour to these meditations; either in reading what I have written respecting it, or of thinking on the tree itself.

The Invocation

ADOL-RWNG-FA! To get the right expression of this word, fancy it being spelled thus: Adol-roong-va. Go over it seven times. At an age like the present, when the epidemic of suicides are on the increase, it becomes you to make use of this soul remedy.

THE CHURCHYARD YEW

Revered reminder of ages long fled!
Thy shade is sacred, beneath lie the dead;
Those wrecks are the relics of mortality,
Their ashes now pay their tribute to thee.

Emblem of sadness! In thy ever dark-green
I trace reflections of a life that has been;
A life all dependent on what is most frail,
At night 'midst thy branches I hear a wail;
It is an echo: the wave-crest: the foam,
A life that is houseless, just driven from home.

In vision I see thee 'mid wilds in the past,
Defiantly braving the rude winter blast
Those winds blow o'er moor and o'er fen,
Places then free from the dwellings of men.

O'er those rude scenes the winds whistled wild,
It is thus how nature nurses her child.
How fragile so-ever the sapling may be,
'Tis doomed to a shaking ere it grows to a tree.

At present 'tis not so much that is seen
Of this sombre old tree, which stands between
The past and the present, the old and the new,
That I am concerned with and telling to you;
But rather 'tis this: the truth I'm revealing,
The Yew is a healer, its powers of healing
Surpasses the body, it extends to the soul!
O poor and dejected, wilt thou be made whole?

Why should you suffer such anguish of mind,
And ever be seeking for what you can't find?
Drugs and potations, all fail to control
Those greatest afflictions, those ills of the soul.
Turn thy sad soul to this grand old tree
Be earnest, be faithful, and thou shalt be free.

This is the sigil   The word for
of the   invocation is
Yew Tree.   ADOL-RWNG-FA.

THE MOUNTAIN ASH
(*Pyrus Aucuparia*)

THIS IS ANOTHER OF THOSE TREES WITH WHICH ALL WHO HAVE HAD THE PRIVILEGE OF LIVING IN THE COUNTRY, OR WHO HAVE EVEN NOTICED THOSE WOODED SHADES WHICH SURROUND THE DWELLINGS OF THE RICH, MUST HAVE BEEN ACQUAINTED WITH. IT IS ONE OF THE MOST BEAUTIFUL TREES WHICH ADORN THE BANKS OF RUNNING STREAMS; OR THAT CLIMBS THE GIDDY HEIGHTS OF MOUNTAINOUS DISTRICTS; OR THAT ORNAMENTS THE PUBLIC HIGHWAYS IN RURAL districts. This plant belongs to the Apple family. Its botanical name is *Pyrus Aucuparia*. It is a plant that will grow at an altitude of nearly three thousand feet above the level of the sea, at the same time it can adapt itself to the richer soil of the warm and fertile lowlands. Its leaves are what Botanists call *Quasipinate*, which means, that the leaves form a shape which much resembles a feather. These pair's of serrated (saw-like) leaflets

161

are from four to six inches long. The flower is cream-coloured; the fruit is globular, orange at first, afterwards scarlet.

There are three stages in the annual changes of this plant; May and June it is green and loaded with cream-coloured bloom which loudly makes known the joy of its youth. After this there are nearly two months during which period it may be said to have no special comeliness. But when September dawns on us the fruitage of the Mountain Ash becomes conspicuous; afterwards that blush of rich vermilion which cannot fail to attract the dullest and most indifferent of observers. These bunches of scarlet berries are generally so profuse as to make this tree conspicuous at a considerable distance. The berries are harmless and full of juice which is intensely acid. All that I know as to the medical properties of this tree is: it was customary with the farmers in my native country, when I was a boy, to press out the juice of the berries and bottle it, to give calves for a complaint which the people called the gurr; I am inclined to consider this word taken from gurgle, as this complaint in the calf resembles diarrhoea in the human, and that of the worst type. I also know that this rarely ever failed to cure such cases.

This tree had another and occult property, with which the people in my country were acquainted; this was: it was considered an antidote to demoniacal influences; or the ill wishes of bad people or black magicians. A portion of this tree was considered fortunate to be kept in the house, also in the out buildings where the cattle were. It was a very common thing for farmers to make a wyth of the twigs of the Mountain Ash, to put about the necks of calves and other creatures, to preserve them from a complaint called the 'strike.' This was sudden death from a stoppage in the circulation. If a farmer wanted a rod to drive his creatures, he generally, if convenient, preferred a branch from this tree. All this would now be called superstition, and simply the result of ignorance, which is at this day supposed to have abounded at that time; for how could it be otherwise, seeing there were no board schools then, nor parish and county councils to look after the people and spend their surplus cash! It is almost a miracle, one would suppose, that people could then live at all, and that in the absence of all our modern fads and schemes of plunder. But they did live, and the farmers prospered very differently to what they do at this day. Whatever may be now called superstition, that superstition must have had a foundation in fact. Although these observances I have been alluding to might be characterised as being very ridiculous; in the meantime there is a truth which underlies this seeming folly which it will be my duty to bring to the light; and when I have made known all I am conscious of respecting this tree, it is possible you may feel more leniently disposed towards those men and women with their simple faith in the virtues of the Mountain Ash.

One night, whilst musing on my bed over a case of gout that had come under my notice, and for which I wanted to find an antidote on the soul plane; it was not long before the Mountain Ash came before my vision; and, in the meantime, before any further looking into the pathological property of this tree, my mind turned spontaneously on the cause and nature of this very terrible complaint. I am fully aware that medical men are not quite agreed as to the primary cause of gout. It has been, I believe, taken for granted, by several of the old school, that it is the result of a redundancy of acid getting into the circulation; a kind of leakage of Uric acid which should otherwise have passed away by way of urine. Others of the profession do oppose this theory, and affirm that acid has little or nothing to do, as a factor, in this complaint; but that it is a species of nervous affection, having characteristics peculiar to itself, which however depends on physiological idiosyncrasies promoted or sustained by habits in which the patient may have indulged; these habits being not necessarily confined to eating and drinking and that exclusively. So far as I have been able to diagnose this complaint, by my soul powers, I may say that there is much truth in both of the fore-mentioned theories. The chief mistake appears to be that neither have gone far enough, each of the parties have stopped at the portals. I will in this paper offer a few remarks which may be taken up by the profession, and applied scientifically, as they have the opportunities of doing so; by which the truth of what I herein write may be tested.

In the first instance I discover an acid in the blood. I am not able to say what this acid may be, I do not think it is Uric acid, but may owe its existence to a combination of such acids as are in the food we eat, and the different liquids we drink. I know such combinations do afford the conditions for the development of an acid whose specific gravity is not so pronounced. I name this Neuro-toxic acid.

When this is produced in the blood it dissolves, or destroys, the red corpuscles; as a result of this destruction, a peculiar lymph is generated in place of the red corpuscles. This lymph is an acrid poison, yet not of so virulent a character as to take away the life of the sufferer at once, unless this lymph finds its way into some of those vitals parts of the body where its effects may be more speedily developed.

It is when connected with the nerve tissues that it does the greater mischief. It is very dangerous when connected with the organs of respiration. But when it reaches the brain, unconsciousness, or lasting idiotcy, or sudden death, is the result.

Many a supposed death from apoplexy may safely be attributed to this complaint. I can safely say that there is no medicine yet discovered that can effectively grapple with this malady. The MOUNTAIN ASH has come before me as having something in itself, either negatively or positively, by which this poison may be nullified. There is in the psychic nature of this plant an occult property which is negative to the pains of Gout, and which can attract to itself that virulent aura, and thereby eventually, take away this complaint.

Whatever may be said respecting the supernatural, there is nothing after all outside nature. What is nature but the workshop of the Infinite! Everything in nature is the subject of a force, and is also capable of transmitting a force. In the meantime not that identical force which it receives; simply because each subject becomes a chemical laboratory peculiarly its own, where, by virtue of those mysterious, because complicated, appliances it does generate another force, unlike that which it receives. I will illustrate this matter: An Alkaline substance becomes the recipient of an acid. What is the force generated? A Salt or a Saline. This Saline is unlike both of its factors.

The Infinite has innumerable hosts of agents in this great workshop, and the subjects of his power are just as innumerable.

Each of these receive, through certain agencies, a force which comes from the Spirit Absolute, through the psychical. Seeing there is nothing higher than Spirit: God is a Spirit; there is nothing lower than what I call the objective material universe. And seeing these are all related, these are all within the domain of nature; where then lies the possibility for the supernatural?

I have in the above remarks pointed out the basis of my Philosophy. I now proceed to particularise. The Mountain Ash is a natural object, it exists in this Great Workshop of the Infinite. It is the recipient of a force. By virtue of this peculiar force, this tree is not some other tree. By virtue of this force the leaves of the Mountain Ash are serrated; the bloom is orange coloured; the berries, when ripe, are scarlet. It is by virtue of this primal force that these same flowers have a perfume peculiarly their own; and that the taste of the fruit is intensely acid. In the meantime, none of these properties are to be found in the Primal force. What is here related belongs, or pertains, to the outward; these are merely what can be sensed by us with one of three senses: The Sight, the Smell, or the Taste. But we have other senses which are prior, and stand higher than the outward ones, and any power that effects the Soul senses is sure, ultimately, to affect the bodily organism.

For hundreds of years past, the sensitives of my own country, have been able to appreciate an influence emanating from this tree unlike that of any other. In my vision I see an old Bard, sitting in the summer months, beneath the shade of the Mountain Ash.

He falls asleep, and in that sleep he dreams that an Angel comes to him, and tells him to arise and convey to his neighbours, the glad tidings, that the tree under which he sleeps, and which is growing on their mountains, and in their forests, and, which all knew so well, had a virtue beyond that of any other plant. That by making a Wyth of its branches, in a circle, and by hanging it up over the entrance door of the house, no evil influence, from witch or spirit, could enter that house. That by placing the same about the neck of a creature, would prevent it from any accident, or from evil wishes; that if they made a cross of two small branches, with the leaves, beneath the head in bed, that the sleeper would have true and important dreams, or revelations from God.

But he gives no instructions about the berries, save this: that evil influences may come from many a source; that is: influences which would prove evil to persons under certain conditions, but which would be harmless in the absence of such conditions.

Some pride themselves in their supposed attainments in occult knowledge; just test that wisdom beside these researches which I am publishing under the *Psychology of Botany*. If your instincts, fail to conduct you into the spirit which pervades these Revelations. If you fail to appreciate these truths, cease hereafter to consider yourselves Occultists, much less Magicians. Remember this: to become a Magician you must become a student of nature at first hand. I now come to deal with the inner nature of this tree: the influence which it receives from the Occult Spheres, and through those Divine Agents which stand graduatedly between the cause and the effect, is intensely blue; this falls on what I will designate an organic structure, that would of itself, subjected to the light of heaven, be a deep dull yellow. By virtue of this soul influence of deep blue falling on the primal molecular substance, an influence is generated, which in its nature is that which pertains to a kind of hidden green!

I will advance no further on these lines beyond this: that this tree, on its occult side, is capable of attracting to itself, and afterwards of retaining in itself, that poison, which I call, and that on my own authority, Neuro-toxic acid, which is the direct cause of the agonies of Gout.

Directions

After sunset, get some one to cut off a twig of the Mountain Ash, sufficiently pliable. Keep your design to yourself, if possible, and with this in view, do all with your own hands, if able.

If the evil be in the lower limbs, put the twig around it for twelve hours, touching the skin. Afterwards, cut the twig up in short lengths and bury them deep in the ground, and as the cut up fragments decay the complaint will pass away.

But for those who call use their will power, and who are able to think of this tree in its absence, to such I give the following advice: After the hour of sunset, and before midnight, place yourself in an easy position as possible; fix your thoughts on this plant; possibly you may know where one grows. Think of the Mountain Ash, and go over the following word eight times:

AV—RUTH—EL.

Do this for eight days, and the pain will be no more.

A SONNET
TO THE MOUNTAIN ASH

Grand tree of trees, that lives and grows,
On mountains bleak amid the snows;
As on yon' bank by placid brook,
In which thy scarlet berries look;

For tho' that stream does onward pass,
It serves for thee a looking-glass;
On which, in ecstasy and bliss,
Thy branches sometimes press a kiss,
When shaken by the Vesper breeze,
Which sings at eve among thy leaves.
Dear Mountain Ash! I love thee well,
Many a secret thou could'st tell!
And when I learn some more of thee,
Greater wonders I shall see.

WOOD NYMPHS

The only plea I offer for writing this strange subject is: it being naturally allied to the *Psychology of Botany*, I consider I should not be doing justice to the one, if I omitted the other.

It will be asked: and do you believe in the existence of such a class of beings? My reply is that I do. I am, and have been for many years, acquainted with this order of intelligences. I will now give you the result of this acquaintance, which constitutes a portion of my Psychological Experiences. Having seen such Beings in the same way that I have seen or sensed other Psychic entities; I have no more reason for doubting their existence than I have for that of any other phenomenon, whose veracity has been proved. These beings resemble, to a degree, the trees to which each one may be allied. Their limbs in many instances resembling the branches of those trees. They possess great powers of fascination; and when they come near a person whose soul is receptive, they impart a feeling of awe. By such a feeling a psychic person may ascertain their presence.

This will be very marked in such as are endowed with a considerable amount of veneration. Such a person, in the midst of a forest, surrounded by large trees, will feel, if calm, that he is in the Temple of the Most High! A feeling of adoration creeps over him. Here you find the primal reason for worshipping in Groves and forests, which temples were coeval with that primal Temple, as the first of all Temples consisted of a clear flat open space, circumscribed by pillars of uncarved stone, with nothing over head but yonder heaven of unchanging blue!

These Wood Nymphs have great powers, either to help or to injure man or beast. Although they cannot communicate with us after the ordinary mode, yet they are, to some extent, affinitized to our race; but more especially those who are in sympathy with some particular tree. When a person is in sympathy with a tree, he is necessarily in sympathy with the Genius of that tree. There are various orders of Wood Nymphs, as there are different orders of plants or trees. See my article on the Yew tree. I saw a host of small beings imbibing the Celestial

Nectar! That is the order of Nymphs which belongs to that tree.

I feel that the time is come for a systematic development of this most interesting branch of the Occult. It may be asked: Why I did not begin this work at an earlier date? My answer is: I had but scant sympathy in my struggles during the past; and it must be borne in mind that Psychics are sensitive, consequently, coldness, or even indifference, is but too quickly felt. Having recently had several very encouraging letters from a number of my subscribers in this country, America, and Australia; I am, in consequence, inspired with fresh vigour in the present work.

You have been made familiar with a portion of God's works in the domain of organic, and inorganic nature: Life under its numerous aspects accosts you at every turn, and from every point of view. There are none, whose experience is so contracted as to be shut out entirely, from a knowledge of some portion of animated nature. You are each acquainted with a number of the animals, and vegetables, which abound.

In the meantime, you are not so presumptuous as to fancy you have seen every plant, every flower, or every creature of every kind that live and move on the earth. You must know, that there are those who have seen more than you, yet, were you to ask the most advanced Naturalist if he had seen every species of animated nature, I feel certain his reply would be: However much I may have seen I have no reason to suppose that I have seen the whole; on the contrary, I have every reason to think I have not acquainted myself with but what lies on the outermost fringe, of that nature, whose limitations are unsearchable. This same holds true in every case, and would be admitted by Naturalist and Philosopher, as no one dare say that he has conversed with every class of animal life; every species of Infusoria; every form of insectorial existence; every crawling reptile; every quadruped; every biped; every bird of every plumage. No, there is not one within the shackled form of 'Old Mortality,' who may lay claim to this Omniscience. Such being the case, who dare to say that what I believe to exist is a myth?

The next item in my belief in this matter is: that there is an influence emanating from each plant or tree, and that when a person thinks intently on any one of these, he, or she, brings himself, or herself, in sympathy with that plant or tree.

This same grand, or sublime law, holds true in our relationship to every other object in nature, from the most distant star in the Milky way, to any one of those brilliants, called 'precious stones,' which are set in the crown of the monarch; the coronet of a Prince; or which may illumine the brow of a Marchioness. Each of these possess an influence, an influence peculiar to its own nature, and which may be utilised by the man who possesses the necessary wisdom.

It is not safe to rush into such spheres, without being previously fortified with a knowledge of the nature of that thing whose influence you may be seeking to realise

I am able to testify, in the support of this verdict, and that in several instances. A case in point: A few weeks ago, whilst diagnosing the hidden properties of the Mountain Ash, I was taken ill. The illness appeared to be located, chiefly, in the stomach and bowels, producing very unusual sensations.

The stomach appeared all on the move, and the bowels became deranged, and diarrhoea set in, the stomach became abnormally distended, and that to such a degree as to give me some alarm. I discontinued my researches, and those horrid symptoms began to subside. In a day or two I resumed my subject, and the same symptoms returned, but not with as much virulency. After a brief truce, I again made an attack, but under new conditions, I fortified myself, thus from my entrenched position I was able to continue my work without further molestation.

You may thus see, it is not safe for a Pioneer in the Occult to push himself, without due precaution, into those unknown departments of nature, where influences may abound, of so baneful a nature as to take away the life of the heedless intruder.

People say to me: 'if I had your powers of vision I would look into everything far and near; I would probe all mysteries; I would unravel enigmas; I would diagnose the nature of the numerous suns which revolve in space.' I can assure you, that you would very soon find that there was a penalty awaiting, and which would have to be paid even to the uttermost farthing for such an inquisitorial disposition. When I made up my mind to probe to the centre of this globe, it took me a long time to do so; simply, that when I followed up this psychic labour even but for a short time, I became exhausted, and that to a fearful degree; for, whilst examining those mysterious Spheres, and awful Spaces, and that but for a short time; I invariably became exhausted, accompanied with, or attended by, a feeling of depression, such as but few have experienced, and that whilst engaged with the ordinary avocations of life. Hence, there is not a plant or tree that I ever diagnose, but what produces sensations in my body, by which I am able to define the psychic, and medicinal properties of the plant or tree. Therefore, what I perceive, in consequence of my developed sensibilities, as an influence, emanating from a tree, leads to the conclusion that others are the subjects of these same influences although they may not be conscious of it.

But, in addition to what may be considered personal experience, I have instances from several of my friends, corroborating what I here make known; nor have I any reason to doubt, but a many more could supplement all this with their additional testimony, did they but feel disposed to do so. I may even advance a step further: each one capable of understanding what he reads could bear his or her testimony to the truth of what is contained in these revelations, and that by way of corroboration, were he convinced as to the importance of such testimony.

I shall, in the next place, promulgate one more great truth, which is, like preceding revelations, the offspring of my own experience, viz.: That there are Beings; semi-intelligent entities, who stand between us and those subtle properties or auras of Plants, Trees, or Minerals. And that such intelligences are capable of enhancing, or retarding those influences we may be seeking to procure.

I presume you will consider this subject as something more than a mere supposition; that it must be a fact; that every Plant or Tree has its own Nymph, who clings to that tree as its own, and is in fact the guardian angel of that tree, and consequently, considers that tree its own property. Thus it is that no one may be able to procure such aura, on the soul plane, by forcible means.

You may thus see the reasonableness of the invocative ritual implied in the word I attach to each plant or tree. In most instances it has been a simple word; in other instances it has been a compound term. It does not follow that such word should be of Greek, Hebrew, Sanskrit or of Welsh derivation, or yet of any other language, known, or unknown. But each word is so formulated that it may express on the physical, or outer plane, such an idea as is expressed on the soul plane.

This is an idea; this idea is an entity; that entity is a force; that force is of such a character as to act directly on portions of these nymphine or intermediate agencies, so as to fascinate them; they thus, for a time, and that to a degree proportionate to their powers of receptivity, combined with a modicum of intelligence, so as to become interested in the wants and feelings of the person who may be in sympathy with the object of their reverence and adoration; and finally, these Nymphs, or intermediates, will consider it to be to their advantage to assist a mortal with their services, on their own plane, and within a circumscribed sphere of operation.

To advanced Occultists, it is well-known, that these Nymphs protect some of the most profound secrets in nature. Whilst making use of the phrase "secrets of nature," it must be understood I am making no special allusion to the far away, either in the heaven above, or in the earth beneath, or in the waters under the earth. These secrets exist in the dew-drop as well as the ocean. They live in the tiny Moss, as majestically as in the Oak, or the stately Cedar of Lebanon. Yet further: Listen to a Sage:

> Could'st thou O man discover what a Moss contains
> Thee it would shock, — 'twould overturn thy brains.
> Those things thou callest great on the outer plane,
> Are not the truly great—just think o'er this again.
> The voice of God is "Small" 'tis also called "Still,"
> 'Tis under such conditions God reveals His will.

The above six lines — which are not the product of a mortal brain — contains the essence of all that is worthy of the name of Philosophy.

You may thus see that all you require is nigh you, it is close at hand. A few of these, by way of specimens, I am continually bringing under your notice in these pages. I seek to conduct you towards the portal of the true Occultism: The Temple of the Infinite!

When we speak or write of these Intermediates, we very readily entertain conceptions of some particular forms or shapes; it appears an impossibility to think of any being or thing without doing so. Thus, whilst writing on this subject, I perceive forms.

At the same time, not such forms as will harmonize with your conceptions. As a rule, we form our estimate of intelligences of every grade by the human model; this limitation arises from the fact that you are not acquainted with intelligences clothed in any other garb, than that of the "human form Divine."

When you think of an Angel, or Spirit, or of any other being capable of giving proofs of intelligence, beyond what is erroneously called instinct, you think of the human, and you anticipate every species of soul phenomena pertaining to the Apparitional, it is the human that crops up, possibly greatly modified.

All this is the result of false teaching, giving you such contracted views, the result of but a very partial enlightenment. In the true sense, an intelligence is not necessarily environed with any special shape or form. There is not a creature of any kind, on this earth, however repulsive it may be to our superficial sense of propriety, but is a development of an intelligence. And if you could, but for a moment, so far transpose your intelligence so as to be conditioned for the sphere of that particular creature, retaining that individual consciousness of your superior sphere of life; you would find as much intelligence in the sphere of that creature as you possess in your fancied superior condition. Yes, far more, as each insect even, however small or insignificant it may be, has a better, or a more complete knowledge — excuse the term — of its own sphere than man has of his.

Mankind dabble in a host of things, the greater portion being but playthings, mere toys.

When pompous science has captured something new, its devotees make as much ado over the find as a young hen does over her first egg. At the same time, in many instances, such a discovery will never contribute the merest fraction towards making the race better, wiser, or happier. Do the multitude comprehend their sphere as perfectly as the Bee or the Ant? Intelligence is neither more nor less than the inspiration of the Almighty. This inspiration when beheld in the lower orders of creation you have been taught to denominate instinct; in man the same faculty you call intelligence, or inspiration.

Nymphs are the true children of nature, partaking of a portion of the physical and psychical. They possess a knowledge of their sphere, which we in this state cannot attain to, save by their agencies.

Science seeks to attain to those hidden mysteries by its puerile researches, but hitherto without success, at least there have been no satisfactory results; for when partial success appears to have been achieved, some dire calamities have followed; nor will it ever be known the amount of evil that has been entailed by such; for if people persist on intruding into these domains; if presumptuous man will poach on the preserves of these conservative agents of nature's subtle forces, he must expect disaster. You readily may see that there is no new discovery of science, however promising its pretensions, but what has opened a door for fresh evils to visit and curse this earth. Pride and avarice are the two chief of devils that are making a hell of this once grand world, and these two are the inspirers and prompters in every new discovery, and in every fresh enterprise.

It is true that these two may develop their identity under distinctive colours, but after all, although two personalities, but one in essence. If mankind would listen to nature's teachings they would find all good.

The Nymph and Sigil of the Mountain Ash.

The Nymph of the Mountain Ash knows more of that tree than any scientist may ever be able to attain to, and that by experimentation or by his unaided observation. Being, as to' myself, on a different plane of life to most of mankind in this respect, I offer you a few crumbs which have fallen from my "master's table."

For your edification and not for your amusement, I make known to you the following:–

The Nymph of the Mountain Ash has a form, that form has a colour, that form is an intelligence, that intelligence has its own sphere, and its own sphere is this its own tree. As to form, I will now presume to define that strange being as I would that of any being on this physical plane; but will give such symbol as came before my vision: See sigil as per diagram. This consists of two triangles, the one inverted, the apex pointing downward; the other, the apex pointing upward, the extreme points of each meeting.

The upper triangle is smaller than the lower one. The upper one is red; the lower one is blue.

THE ALDER TREE
(Ae'nus Glutinoso)

THIS TREE BELONGS TO THE BIRCH, OR CATKIN BEARING FAMILY. THERE ARE SOME SIXTY OR SEVENTY SPECIES OF THIS FAMILY SCATTERED THROUGHOUT THE WOODS OF EUROPE AND NORTH ASIA, THE COMMON ALDER BEING ONE.

THIS TREE HAS SEVERAL NAMES BY WHICH IT IS KNOWN IN THE DIFFERENT PARTS OF THIS COUNTRY. IN THE WELSH LANGUAGE IT IS called Pren Gwrn, or Pren Wrn. It is also known as the Wollar tree. The name for this tree in Cheshire is Owlar. I am not conversant with any other of those provincial cognitives which must exist. In the meantime, I do not think that any reader will fail to recognise this tree when I say that it grows beside brooks, stagnant pools, and swamps and boggy places, such are the situations where it thrives best; at the same time, it will not refuse to grow in dry places, and along road sides. This is one of those trees which is but little noticed, nor do I find but very few remarks respecting it in Botanical works, much less in Medical.

When viewed as an object of interest on the outer plane it is not prepossessing; there is nothing attractive to the casual observer. It is dull, dark and ungainly, it does not display the beauty and loveliness of other members of this family, such as the Oak, the Birch, the Poplar, and the Willow.

This sombre inhabitant of the morass appears fretful and peevish, and gives one the impression of one who is weighed down with grief and sorrow. One whose cruel treatment and general neglect had begotten in its outer nature the sourness of a misanthrope. Yet in spite of this repulsiveness, its inner bark is a good astringent for a relaxed stomach and bowels in man or beast, this I have proved for a number of years. When a boy, I have known men whose feet had become chafed by perspiration and travel, gathering the leaves of the Alder Tree, and applying them to parts that were even bleeding at the time, who have afterwards resumed their journey without the previous agony. You may thus see that this gloomy tree is not destitute of virtue, notwithstanding its morose appearance. But, as you already know, outward appearances are not always the safest of guides, this I shall be able to make clear to you in the present revelation of the Alder tree, in its occult and psychic properties as discovered by me on the soul plane. Here I find virtues of no ordinary type. In fact the word extraordinary would best comport with those ideas of which I am made acquainted.

An Occultist looking at the characteristical Sigil or Symbol of those occult forces possessed by this tree will not fail to discover what the Medical Botanist has not even the most remote idea of.

I would here make a statement, and that at the outset, that this tree possesses magical virtues! and like the Mountain Ash is capable of producing extraordinary results. At the same time, the disparity between these two trees is very great. There is, in fact, a chasm between both that cannot be bridged over so as to unite or reconcile the both natures.

The Mountain Ash is governed by Mars in the sign Leo. The Alder tree is governed by Saturn in the sign Scorpio! You will readily see from these positions that the disparity is great indeed, at the same time, the magical power of each when employed on its own line, and within its own limits or sphere, is overwhelmingly great, grand, and glorious. But, by way of caution, I would say that these strange forces must not be played with by the novice who may never have studied such occult laws, or who may not have graduated in the realm of soul.

A person may make use of the bark, leaves, or roots with impunity, and that, in many instances with advantage, so long as he deals but with the outer tree and that on the material plane, a thing which anyone may use or cut up, according to his wants or his caprice, and that to his heart's content, as in such a case he is dealing with but the shadow.

However, this is not the case when he has to do with that world of realities, the domain of forces, the sphere of causation, that realm of celestial activities where causes are in continual operation, producing on the outer plane the phenomenal universe.

It was the language of a primitive Christian, who was also an Apostle, that he "looked not at the things which are seen, but at the things that are not seen." At first sight this passage appears a self contradiction, for how could a person look at what is unseen? It simply implies the two-fold nature of man in his relationship with that two-fold universe of which he is a part. The inner world and the outer world; the inner sight and the outer sight; one adapted for the other.

The Apostle addressed his pupils from the platform of an Occult Philosopher. The things that are seen are temporal or transient, but the unseen verities which are realised by the inner sight are eternal.

Those forces which produce the outer phenomenal tree cannot be destroyed by the woodman's axe. It is true the tree as such, exists no longer, but the few remaining roots may shoot forth a new stem, or the seed from that tree may be carried away by some gust of wind to some genial spot where it may fructify by virtue of that power belonging to that plant, and thus once more, that power builds up or materializes another tree in the likeness of the parent tree which has been cut down. It is to this same elemental plane I am directing your attention; and that sigil is the symbol of that power belonging to the Alder.

He who has wisdom may here find information above and beyond anything ever before published. All that is secret in this figure must remain so, as no one but the initiate will understand, and all I have met with are too clever to learn, so let each grope out his own way whilst I scatter abroad pearls of great value, and he who has eyes to see will gather them.

The Analysis

I will, in the present instance, make known a few of those mysteries which are made known to me on the soul plane, and which I publish to the world. Glorious truths, such as this race has not heard of since the dawn of history.

In the first place, the influence of this tree is of an isolating character. It tends to break up old associations, or old and intimate relationships, and that from the time a person or thing comes under this influence. Thus any excrescence, tumour, or any substance whatever joined psychically with this influence must inevitably pass away, from that moment you disconnect that substance on the soul plane it begins to operate on the physical plane, which will ultimately appear. In the second place, this influence has a reconstructing power; it not only effects the end of one thing, but also the beginning of another; on the one hand there is a death, on the other hand there is a birth. Thus out of apparent evil comes real good; or rather evil is succeeded by a good, yet not under the same conditions. Thus the influence of this tree if brought to bear on one's present life would disconnect one from the life of the past, and the mind would become disqualified for the occupations of the past, and, unless the mind had been previously prepared for soul work, the life of such a one would become a blank, he would appear to be non-progressive and all would end. This influence brought to bear on an imbecile would break up the old conditions, and the future would be altogether new.

At the same time, there is no certainty as to how, or to what extent such may operate; hence it is not safe to apply this power to any other purposes than the destruction of excrescences, tumours, long-standing ulcers, or any local complaint, but it would not be safe to apply such a force to the bodily constitution in any way.

These powers may prove an advantage to the hermit or recluse, as its disconnecting influence would take away from him any remaining longings for companionship which might be lurking within his mind. And further, it gives or enhances that aversion to all that the world calls brilliant or glorious. It would render a person not only apathetic to the busy outside world life, but begets a positive hatred towards everything on this outer plane, so that there is nothing, however fascinating, that could prove a charm to one allied to this terrible power, neither music, or painting, or any of the productions of human genius; in fact, the very objects in nature, and of nature herself would prove unattractive, or would be lost sight of. The great world itself like a moving panorama, recedes, it disappears. The grand unseen, the soul world alone opens to his eyes, his auditory powers on the inner plane become vibrant, as the winds from the unseen shore waft dulcet harmonies which awakes the Æolian harp within those mystic depths, and that for the first time.

Such realities await the man who has lived, laboured and suffered whilst climbing the hill, ever reaching out his hand to grasp the unseen. Those influences of the Alder tree would apply beneficially to the character I have been describing. The word of invocation is CED–RAGEL (pronounced Ked).

This is the sigil
of the
Alder Tree.

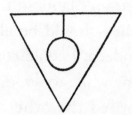

The word for
invocation is
CED–RAGEL.

This word should be repeated seven times, deliberately, and with reverential feelings, having the Sigil before you at the time.

THE ELDER TREE
(Sambucus-nigar)

THIS IS SAID TO BELONG TO THE HONEYSUCKLE FAMILY. SUCH CLASSIFICATIONS WERE FOUND ABSOLUTELY NECESSARY, OR THE STUDY OF BOTANY, AS A SCIENCE, COULD NEVER BE EFFECTIVELY ACCOMPLISHED. THUS IT WAS FOUND NECESSARY THERE SHOULD BE ORDERS, CLASSES, TRIBES, OR FAMILIES.

IT DOES NOT NECESSARILY FOLLOW THAT THOSE WHO HAVE LAID DOWN, FOR OUR GUIDANCE SUCH AND SUCH RULES and have described certain plants so that we may be able to identify them, that they should be always correct in their descriptive writings. Indeed, I could contradict some of these writers were it worth my while to do so.

I was greatly surprised the other day, whilst reading a paragraph by Dr Carpenter on the medical, and other properties of the Elder Bark, to find him giving to this said bark an astringent property.

See *Vegetable Physiology, and Systematic Botany,* by William Carpenter, M.D.F.R.S. & F.G.S. Page 453, Section 623, he has the following: "The bark is generally astringent; that some species has been used for Tanning; and that of others has been employed in medicine for the same purpose, and with similar effects as Peruvian Bark."

What I have to offer as a set-off to this is : That for the purpose of a brisk purgative and diuretic combined, I never found a better than the decoction of the inner bark of the Elder. (*Sambucus-nigar*). *Is* it possible that a purgative of so pronounced a character should be such an astringent? I have always considered an astringent that which binds together; the very reverse of laxative.

The Elder flourishes in damp smelly places, as well as along road sides. It appears to possess the power of transmuting the corruptible into the incorruptible. It stands between us and the corruptible, it thus constitutes one of natures filters. The word corruption is a relative term; for strictly speaking, truthfully, and philosophically, there is no corruption.

Corruption consists in too much of one element concentrated in one place. The fumes from a putrid carcase is corruption; but when that putrid mass is buried and its offensive fumes are imbibed by a living plant, it becomes transmuted into a living vegetable organism which represents the incorruptible.

Thus, the Elder tree absorbs the offensive effluvia which emanate from stagnant pools and filthy sewers, and thus changes them into life and loveliness.

The charms which this tree possesses are but few; nor is it ever looked on as an object of beauty, the odour it gives is anything but fragrant, nor are the odours from its flowers at all fascinating. But it yields a fruit, which if fully understood, is without a parallel in its several uses among the sick; and its wine is equal to either Port or Sherry. Thus what may be lacking in the beautiful, is more than compensated in the good and the useful.

The Elder is more plentifully distributed in the South of England than the north. I consider this tree a native of Britain, and existed in these parts long before that rupture took place which cut off this land from the continent of Europe. Indeed I may with confidence presume to say that it is one of the oldest fruit bearing trees which this country possesses.

The influences of Venus in the sign Scorpio are allied to the Elder. I furnish you with the Symbol of the elemental powers, and virtues of this tree.

I hope such subjects as I am now giving may prove sufficiently interesting as to induce some to make it a part of their study; and that they may be led to see that there are more "secrets in heaven and earth" than modern scientists have ever dreamed of in their philosophy. I shall here withdraw myself from the outer materialised tree, and will look at this object on the soul plane.

The influences of the Psychic Elder appear to rotate at an inexpressible speed about its mystic centre, which I will, for convenience designate the stem; at the same time this stem becomes absolutely invisible! This invisible centre has a number of minor centres which branch off from the parent stem, and each of these minor branches constitute centres around which a proportionately smaller circle of influences revolve. These influences, successively become absorbed in mysterious vortices, and are lost from view; at least from my view.

But after the lapse of a few months, this whirl of atoms develops into a new phenomenon, consisting in new foliage, new flowers, and new clusters of berries.

I perceive the motion of this whirl, in the first instance, tends downwards towards the root part of the mystical stem, where it passes through a process of infilteration, when it afterwards ascends towards the extremities, having finished its mystic round.

Such is the order of that wonderful evolution on the soul plane, before this tree is beheld on this outer plane; at least, such is what I realise on the inner plane. The seat of all force, the cause of every species of organic life is a vortex, and the centre of that vortex is a vacuum! It is here where dwells the motive energy; the God! Yes, it appears to me at this moment, that what I call a vacuity is the dwelling-place of Omnipotence!

In the next place, this tree on the soul plane, and as witnessed by me from a psychic standpoint, is of a very deep dark purple colour. It therefore represents the feminine side of nature, and is negative to all those matters with which it stands related.

When an Occultist speaks of the Feminine, or the Masculine, it must be borne in mind that such terms are not used by him as distinguishing marks of gender. I know such terms are bandied about very freely — by a number of writers in such a light as to beget very absurd notions respecting this subject, simply because the mind of the writer has failed to grasp the true idea as to what is implied by the terms Masculine and Feminine.

Men go to write on these sublime themes steeped in the filth of their own animality; and with dirty fingers pollute those pages of wisdom found in nature, that book of God, stereotyped in ineffaceable characters on the fiery ether, that ever unfolding Scrowl. But he who has wisdom will detect the sham from the genuine coin.

There is a sham Occultism, and there is a genuine one; the former gives lectures and reconnoitres every city, town, village and hamlet, in his search for proselytes. He seeks publicity in all those fashionable and popular devices now current, and like his prototype, the Pharisee of old, he does all to be seen of men. As a next subterfuge, he slanders the individual, and stigmatises such Divine Inspirations given forth by him with the opprobrious epithet "Obsession." Thus proving descent from those who told the Christ of history to his face that he had a devil. If they, the fathers of modern hypocrites, called the "Master of the house Beelzebub, how much more they of his household."

The genuine Occultist seeks not publicity in order to promote his own popularity, or that of his philosophy. He may be desirous that all should become acquainted with the leading principles of his system of Philosophy, considering such a move a step in the right direction. The true Occultist, conscious of the wealth he possesses in that wisdom, the price of which exceeds that of rubies; he unavoidably feels a species of independency which the riches of this world cannot afford. He feels strong in the truth of his Lord, and in the power of his might, in that he has found the way to that hidden manna. He has opened a fountain in the flinty rock, the water follows him, he has drank of it, it is henceforth within him a well of water, springing up into life eternal.

I make known to you one of the grand mysteries of heaven: It is with the Negative side of Divinity that we have to do. It is the Mother side of Deity, not the Father's side. The negative, not the positive.

The mother does not only embrace her offspring with the arms of her affection, but she feeds it from the breasts of her consolation. Thus it is that whilst we are the offsprings of nature, and are dandled on her knees, she bountifully meets our numerous and diversified wants with profusion from her exhaustless stores. In miniature, I discover in the Elder a very appropriate type of that phase of providence to which I have been alluding.

This tree is negative, hence it possesses properties, or rather attributes, as I view such organic forms as living agencies, and not as a conglomeration of dead matter, moved mechanically by some extraneous influences. So long as you look but at the outer form of the Elder, you will fail to appreciate those higher aspects, those more subtle virtues, which live immortally in this beautiful Symbol, which through the Divine aid I have exhumed from the buried past.

Again: To what phase of human nature does this tree ally itself, so as to prove of value? The answer to this question arises spontaneously as I now write it: Persons of gross habits, and where there may be a tendency toward vices of a low and animal character. Such persons may be relieved from an intolerable burden, a burden which if hugged and carried will ultimately weigh its possessor down to the gates of death. "For he who sows to the flesh, shall of the flesh reap corruption." And this corruption is the second death.

The Elder tree, on the soul plane, is capable of absorbing those influences which do fire the passions of those who are constitutionally exposed to such influences. It must ever be borne in mind that every species of vice originates in a disease, which produces soul deformity. Whenever a person becomes abnormally developed in any one phase of vice, that man or woman is the subject of a disease; and for every disease in human nature, Nature has a cure. If our Philanthropists and Legislators were to pay attention to this; were half those funds, which now support Christian missions, devoted to the support of men who might be competent to receive and carry out these great truths which I could teach them, crime itself in a few generations might become extinct. But they will not heed any remarks from me; and they will go on with their hanging and imprisonments.

Here I offer freely a cure for one of the most prominent vices of this day: the vice of lust and animality. Turn your thoughts to this purple mother tree. She will absorb that pernicious poison which has become engendered in thy nature O man, and will convey it downwards where the poison becomes changed; it is there transmuted, and rendered capable of yielding to thee during the rest of thy life the beautiful flowers and fruits of rightness.

Some there are, who may consider these teachings as being but the wild hallucinations of an enthusiast; one who may be supposed to have been long a denizen in the domain of imagination, so as to have become intoxicated with those delusive dreams, which, like those fascinating exhalations which is said to have, at one time, ascended from the Pythian spring. But, what a sublime satisfaction it is to know that what the superficial thinkers, and writers, may understand by the epithet "imagination," as being equivalent to a vagary, the Occult Philosopher has made the very important discovery, that this tabooed region of imagination, is after all: the world, yes, the Universally Real.

The intellect alone, when uninspired, moves within a radius of a very contracted circle; and within these limits, the unaided intellect gets bewildered with those numerous enigmas which beset it on every hand.

After all those laborious researches, those testings and probings, and analytical siftings; when the diligent investigator is about to congratulate himself on his achievements, he may feel disposed to consider himself most fortunate, seeing he has attained to that long looked for consummation. In the midst of all this, he finds he has a successor, a rival, whose discoveries on those same lines, overturns the facts and theories of previous discoveries.

But the man whose intellect is illumined with the true light of heaven has no cause to fear that any one who may take up these same subjects on these same lines, will ever be in a position to say that what I have written is false. It is true, another mind may, at some future period appear on the scene, who may see more than I have seen, and who may express those lucid visions in loftier phrases. Yet, what I have written is written, and will never be obliterated.

If the men and women of this generation choose to put these facts of mine to the test, I have no doubt but results will prove satisfactory, providing the conditions be complied with. The Occult Name of the Elder Tree. HOO–VAH–MAH.

This is the sigil
of the

Elder Tree.

The word for invocation
is

HOO–VAH–MAH.

THE BIRCH TREE.
(Betula'ceœ)

THIS IS ANOTHER OF THE CATKIN TRIBE, OR FAMILY; AND IS AS BEAUTIFUL A TREE AS ANY WHICH GROWS IN A WILD STATE IN THIS COUNTRY. ITS SILVERY BARK RENDERS IT A CONSPICUOUS OBJECT IN ARBOREAL SCENERY, AND MAY BE DISTINGUISHED AT A CONSIDERABLE DISTANCE. IT HAS BEEN CALLED BY SOME "THE LADY OF THE FOREST."

THIS IS ANOTHER OF THAT SPECIES OF TREES WHICH ARE NATIVES OF THIS COUNTRY. IT IS ONE WHICH DELIGHTS IN moist or marshy land, and its domain extends the furthest north of any other tree or shrub.

Being a plant so well-known by all, I need not waste time or take up space with further description. I now proceed to notice the planet and sign which are sympathetically related to the

Birch: These are the planet Mercury in the sign Pisces. In the remarks I am here making, and the revelation I am now publishing on the Planetary government of the Birch tree, judged from a Stellar standpoint, I am not consciously expressing what any other person may have said or written. I am simply giving what I find, regardless of the views of others; in the meantime, I respect the views or opinions of others, so far as they prove the outcome of honest conviction, although they may clash with these my findings.

Honesty of research, and purity of purpose, deserve our respect at all times and that under every circumstance, so long as each one gives what he finds and that to the best of his ability. The Birch is a plant which partakes of the nature of Mercury and Jupiter combined. You may readily convince yourself of this by a studious and careful observation.

Mercurial plants, on the whole, are tough, stringy or fibrous, such as is common in the hemp family; in this respect the Birch bears some resemblance to the Hemp tribe. There is yet another property in the Birch which bears a further resemblance to the Hemp, and that is, its stimulating power over the nervous system in general, and the brain in particular.

I know from experience that a decoction of the Birch branches, or what is better, the inner bark which is stronger than the branches, acts very powerfully as a stimulant on the brain. Indeed as the result of my personal experience, I am forced to the conclusion that it very much resembles our grand old household beverage, the cheering cup of Tea.

I have thought, and that repeatedly, that with a little cooking, and by the addition of some light vegetable aromatic, such as may be found in the cowslip bloom, or the petals of the white rose, that a substitute of a very invigorating character, for the ordinary tea might be produced. One thing I know, that the decoction of Birch alone possesses a wonderful power for clearing the head and sharpening the intellect at those times when a sluggishness seems to becloud the mental faculties; and as this is quite harmless, it would, if applied to, prove a boon to thousands. In this the Hemp, as a family, do differ as they are not so safe; moreover the Hemp are more or less laxative and diuretic; the Birch is not laxative but is an excellent diuretic.

There is another feature in the Birch which declares it a partaker of the influence of Jupiter; and this is its white and silvery bark. Jupiter is sympathetic with whiteness combined with brightness, hence block tin is a metal of Jupiter. Further: The sign Pisces is called the night house of Jupiter, and in judicial Astrology, represents moist or marshy land, and boggy places, but not what may be called filthy places; and as the Birch seems partial to such localities, I think it must be an obvious truth that the sign Pisces must have some influence over this tree, for things or properties equal to the same thing must be equal to each other, in a certain sense at least. These are a few of my outward evidences on the planetary government of this tree; I give them, as they may interest those who have some knowledge of Astrology. I sincerely hope that what I have adverted to respecting the natural properties of this tree may induce a few of my friends to a further investigation of such a matter. I should be pleased to receive from any who may have given some attention to this subject, the result of his or her investigations.

I proceed to a further consideration of what I find on that plane with which I may be more conversant than those I am here addressing: It is quite possible I may give something of a very different character to what was afforded my readers respecting the Alder tree. I make this remark simply because Botanists place this tree in the same category as the Alder. Both yield catkins, and the leaves of both are very much alike, and are partial to like situations; further and beyond all this, there is some similarity in the property of the inner bark of each.

On the psychic plane there is a great dissimilarity, which I shall be able to point out ultimately.

The psychic Birch appears in the following garb: The colours are variegated; a blending of Yellow, Green, Pink, and Blue; neither colour very defined, but a shading of one in that of the other, as if the whole were blended into one; at the same time, not with the same effect as that produced by a similar admixture of colours by the art of the painter; in such a mixture there would be a blank indefiniteness, whereas in this psychic phenomenon each colour is distinguishable, yet one species of 'blend.' The apparent unity is real harmony, and the harmony is unity. As a whole the impression is that of softness or a mellowness, exceeding anything of beauty or loveliness on the outer plane of life. Further; this tree on the psychic plane appears more symmetrically formed. It must be ever borne in mind that we must not expect such perfection of organisation on this outer plane as what exists on the inner.

The inner is the ideal; this ideal is the design of the Divine Architect! Here all is perfection! Yes this Divine ideal is the marvellous program given out by the grand First Cause — to those subordinates designated: 'Thrones, Principalities, and Powers'; and however perfect the design might be, the execution of that design, being entrusted to finite intelligences, who must develop with their work, cannot appear so perfect when under these outward adverse conditions as the ideal may be in its absolute condition.

Thus it is, that there is a builder up of every tree, plant, and shrub. Yes, and this builder can paint as no mortal artist may be able to rival.

There is a builder of the Birch tree. The Symbol here given is the Occult Builder of the Birch tree. That Being who works by the ordering of Eternal laws. It is that being, or by virtue of his power that those special elements are collected together, and focalised in the form of this tree, and that according to the grand design and eternal ordination.

Within his own sphere, this servant of the Most High is omnipotent. This servant manifests his wisdom and his power, and his intelligence, in that special outward manifestation; some living organic structure, where is found its ultimate on the outer plane. This Being is not dependent on the organic tree for its existence any more than electricity is dependent on the thundercloud for its existence. The element called electricity is universally distributed, but its development to our sense of vision as a spark, or in the lightning flash, depends on certain conditions; and even these conditions are not the fortuitous jumblings of a purposeless fatuity.

In nature there is no such a thing as a movement of any kind, from the terrible collapse of a world, to the falling of a leaf in Autumn, but is the result of a Power; that power is combined with a degree of intelligence, an intelligence subordinate to a higher one. To me the whole Universe is like a hive, containing beings more active than the "busy bee." Yes, the Universe is one grand Pantheon, each chamber, each niche, each recess, is tenanted by a god; each god is delegated with omnipotence in its own sphere; at the same time, the whole of these gods are controlled by one supreme head.

Such was the most ancient creed of primeval man, at a period when he, in the outward form, could hold communion with these gods; in which sense it was he "walked with the gods," and as the result, he triumphed over the law of disintegration, of which he by nature was a subject.

In the next place, I will make known to you those conditions to which the virtues of the Birch do apply. I feel a degree of certainty, that there are among my readers, a few at least, who will feel grateful for this information.

Restlessness, nervous irritability, accompanied with great anxiety. Direct your thoughts to the Birch, going over the Word and Invocation as here given: AM-VEL-RAH.

O Thou the Absolute Essence; the Unchanging Essence;
the Eternal Essence; the Essence of Quiet; Absolute
Stillness!

Allow this my restlessness to find peace in Thee.

Allow my uncertainties to find absolute certainty in
Thee!

Allow what is fleeting in me to find stability in Thee!

Fill this corruptible body with Thine incorruptibility.

Transmute my weakness into Thy strength.

Transform this mortal into Thine Immortality.

Give to me, a homeless wanderer, an Eternal home in
Thy Divine Essence.

Amen, Amen, Amen!

This is the sigil
of the
Birch Tree.

The word
for invocation is
AM-VEL-RAH.

THE POPLAR TREE
(*Populus Nigra*)

"THE FAMILY OF THE POPLAR COMPRISES NO MORE THAN TWO GENERA., VIZ.: POPULUS, IN WHICH ARE INCLUDED POPLARS OF ALL KINDS; AND SALIX, TO WHICH BELONG THE WILLOWS, THE SALLOWS, AND THE OSIESS." FROM *BRITISH AND GARDEN BOTANY*, BY LEO GRINDON.

THAT SPECIES OF WHICH I AM SPEAKING IN THIS ARTICLE IS WHAT IS KNOWN AS THE BLACK POPLAR, AND IS MORE plentifully distributed than any of the other species. The leaves are larger, and of triangular shape. The branches are numerous and thickly arranged together. It is of rapid growth, and abounds in hedges, road sides, and forests; and is partial to wet or damp bottoms. It is well-known to all who are conversant with country life. The properties of the inner bark are well-known to the medical Botanist.

Both the Moon and Mercury are in sympathy with the Poplar tree, from the fact of it containing influences, or virtues, which do emanate from the planet Mercury when situated in the celestial sign Cancer, which is the house of the Moon. From this fact alone you may presume, that even from a physical point of view, it must abound with virtues, which apply directly, and most beneficially to the most vital parts of the human body; more especially those parts whose action, and healthy continuity of action, depends on the primal matter; which is that pabulum of which the brain and the whole nervous system is composed. I may here state that every species of Poplar contains some little of these virtues, but are not so directly defined, hence not so directly applicable.

As I view this tree on the soul plane, as a psychic phenomenon, its colour is a very deep red approaching a purple shade, that is the stem; whilst what I designate its bloom is a most lovely white, and bears a striking resemblance to that superb flower the Water Lily. I once saw a grand specimen of the Water Lily in an out of the way place, floating in loveliness, and loneliness, on the surface of a deep pit, and I was much impressed with its likeness to what is described as the Lotus. The bloom which adorns the psychic Poplar is like that grand flower; the finest specimens of the water Lily I had ever seen.

The more I contemplate this grand tree, the richer appears its purple, and the more enchanting the rich milky white of its unfading bloom; supported in a gorgeous clayx, which resembles a cup of gold, the edge of which has exfolded tips.

The centre has no signs of procreative seed vessels. Thus the contrast from purple to golden and delicate white is highly fascinating.

The tree does not appear to ascend upward to such a height as its physical counterpart. Its branches stretch out like wings; the top of the tree appearing bulgy, resembling the top of a large balloon. As a whole it appears vibrative with life; every part lives; every part moves. It produces an impression on my mind which renders me unconsciously breathless; as if the act of breathing was not necessary for my life. I have not, within the range of my psychic experience in connection with the *Psychology of Botany*, met with any herb, plant, or tree, or one of the minerals, which possesses so many virtues, having so general an application.

In all cases the cure should begin on the soul plane, as it is on that plane where by far the greater number of complaints originate. You are in the present instance, presented with a remedy already prepared, and that in such an order that its presentation will not raise the gorge, even of the most delicately constituted invalid. Here you have no nauseous draught or bitter potation: it is by thinking and not by drinking. Dwell on this tree in your thoughts, as in all other psychological applications, going over the word and repeating the invocation in all sincerity. In the meantime, if you should be so far engrossed with the material as not to be able to fix your thoughts abstractedly on this subject; if you find yourself unable to devote ten minutes, or a quarter of an hour once or twice a day to this object; the next best thing would be to go to a Medical Botanist, or Herbalist, and ask for the Black Poplar Bark in some of those forms in which such drugs are administered.

I will here furnish you with all those symptoms to which the psychic Poplar does apply: Destitution of the power to will anything, so as to be able to execute anything that may be desirable. The person is so far enfeebled as to be unable to say: I will go for a walk to visit a friend on a certain day, or at a certain hour. No, he cannot do so; he may appear fairly well as to outward appearance; he may be able to partake of his food in the ordinary way; he can move about and converse freely and rationally; he can even do anything which happens to be on those ordinary lines of daily routine, or anything not partaking of the character of a resolution; should it be so, then all is failure. This is a disease, the primal source of which is in the soul. Should any one thus afflicted, cast his or her eyes on these remarks relating to this mode of curing, I fear that this person would fail to apply it. In the meantime, and as I have elsewhere remarked, this may be done by proxy; another may apply this remedy for the patient, even without his knowledge, if such be necessary; and in most cases such secrecy would be necessary, as the person could not be convinced that anything of the kind was needed. But if you are unable to form a resolution so as to will its execution; be assured you are among those that are sick and need a physician.

Another symptom is loss of memory; that is in such a case as where good memory once existed. This will be obvious in the loss of names of persons and places; it is here you find the most ready test in cases where loss of memory is setting in. But even in cases where memory has ever been defective this would improve it. Dullness of apprehension; this is a symptom extensively prevalent, and at the best it is apt to show itself, in a more or less degree, when the prime of life is past. Weak or imperfect eyesight; Deafness, arising from constitutional weakness; also all that class of symptoms which pertain to the digestion, assimilation, secretion, absorption, all those offices requiring the healthy action of the stomach, liver, kidneys, and bowels, the Poplar tree is a remedy.

This is the sigil
of the
Poplar Tree.

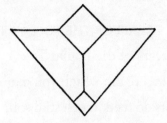

The word for
invocation is
AV—VI—HU—GAL.

Arch-Master of forces!

Author and giver of life.

Master Builder of the Universe.

O thou prime mover, without whose presence nothing
moves; without whose Life nothing lives; without
whose Intelligence nothing thinks; without whose eye
nothing sees; without whose ear nothing hears.

O thou mighty One; O thou ruler of the heaven of
heavens!

It is Thine to reside in the north!

Thy footprints are seen in the south!

With thy right hand thou raisest the Sun from his couch
in the morning; with thy left hand thou puttest him
to sleep beneath the mountains of the west!

Give to my eyes Thy sight.

Give to my mind Thy thoughts.

O Thou author of the light of the morning Sun! place
Thy lamp in my dark soul.

MY DREAM OF THE POPLAR TREE.

O let me dream of the Poplar Tree,

That lives in a realm which you may not see;

Whose roots do feed in celestial soil,

Which has not been curs'd by rapine and spoil;

Where it grows perennial; for ever in bloom;

Such is that bless'd life beyond the tomb!

But what is there now to be said of this tree

Which lives on this earth, where grim misery

In many a shade, 'neath many a fold,

Its imprints are traced among young and old.

Then look to this tree, for here I find

A balm for my brain, and strength for my mind.

For aches and for pains it yields what you need;

'Twill help you on what is immortal to feed.

The way for achievement you all know now,

Just think of the Poplar, its stem, leaf, and bough.

My soul ope's a door to the Poplar unseen,

Whose leaves are of purple, no longer of green;

This tree is the fountain, it yields the supply,

Which flows on for ever,—this Poplar can't die.

And when I'm divested of Mortality,

This tree on the soul plane again I shall see.

THE ELM TREE
(*Ulmus Campestres*)

THIS TREE REQUIRES FROM ME BUT FEW REMARKS OF A DESCRIPTIVE CHARACTER, AS IT IS WELL-KNOWN TO ALL WHO MAY HAVE THE LEAST INTEREST IN THE TREE LIFE OF THIS COUNTRY. AT THE SAME TIME, THERE ARE CHARACTERISTICS PERTAINING TO THIS TREE WHICH SOME READERS OF THIS BOOK MAY NOT BE ACQUAINTED WITH, AND WHICH WOULD BE OF INTEREST TO THEM.

It may be a well-known fact that the upper surface of the leaf is exceedingly rough, it may also be known to all, that the leaves are serrated or toothed, sometimes doubly so. But there is one feature connected with the leaf of the Elm which appears peculiar: the leaf comes down the petiole, or stem, lower on one side than it does on the other. If you look at it from a back or under view, the leaf bends to the lobed side, which is on the left side from the under view. Small reddish-brown flowers appear before the foliage, in this it may not be peculiar, as several of our fruit trees do the same, the Plum, the Cherry, the Apple for instance; nevertheless, the Elm, if studied very carefully, will display certain peculiarities not discoverable in any other tree. The flowers of the Elm appear on the preceding year's twigs. They are globular in form, and sessile — that is, without a stem, and consist of bunches a little over half an inch in length and breadth, which are so abundant as to make the branches appear knotted. They ripen when the climate permits concurrently with the opening foliage, the clusters mingle with the young leaves presenting the appearance of the female Hop flowers.

The Elm family embraces the Sugar Berry or Nettle tree, and the Wych Elm, but it is the common Elm that forms the subject of this article. It does not appear to be indigenous to this country as the seed but rarely ripens sufficiently to propagate itself in the way indigenous plants do. Every indigenous plant is so organised as to be capable of conveying its own seed by the use of wings carried by the wind, or by other agencies to some spot where it may germinate. The birds and small animals instinctively deposit the seed or fruit of plants in the earth, near the surface preparatory for those cold and cruel months, when "there is no fruit on the vine," and when "the labour of the Olive shall cease." These children of nature do not always remember where their deposits lie, — very unlike the genius of this 19th century civilisation, — hence such deposits germinate and grow, as herbs, plants, and trees. It is in this way the seed could be carried and deposited, and thus preserved, but the seed of the Elm not having ripened there can be no germination or growth; so that the evil is attributable to the unsuitability of the climate rather than the ordination of the providence of God.

The Elm is not a Forest tree, it grows in hedges, and along the waysides, also in parks, where it frequently appears to rival the Oak. Sometimes you meet with a magnificent old Elm with its spacious branches situated in one of those squares in old cities. A certain author gives the following:– his name I have not got — "Whether standing alone upon the sward, or marshalled with a hundred others into one of those incomparable green arcades, of which there is no finer example in England than the avenue leading to Redland Court, near Bristol, the grandeur of a full grown Elm never fails to awaken pride in our country's trees, and to light up our hearts with delight and admiration." There is no man or woman, young or old, rich or poor, learned or unlearned, but may derive a special blessing through the study and contemplation of the Elm tree. It will now be my task to make known to you the inner and deeper truths of the psychic, and more sublimely glorious characteristics of the Elm tree.

The Elm Tree on the Soul Plane

It may be necessary to reiterate what I have elsewhere made known, that each plant or tree on this earth had a prior existence on the soul plane; that this is the primal source of everything that lives and grows on this earth plane; each lived the soul life prior to that material life, in which garb it is recognised by us during the present life. It may appear hard for you to receive this truth, but it is worthy of your most ardent researches, as so glorious a realisation will eclipse your most vivid conceptions and will surpass your most enthusiastic anticipations, such contemplations convey to your heart the assurance that there can be no absolute loss in God's Universe. It was most likely such an assurance which inspired an Apostle to exclaim: "For we know that if the earthly house of this tabernacle be dissolved we have a building of God, a house not made with hands, eternal in the heavens." It is only those who are the subjects of such realisations that are the possessors of such assurance, relating to the stability and continuity of life and loveliness.

It is so arranged in God's providence, that when the mortal eye is closed by death, and can no longer look on nature's beautiful landscapes on this side the dark river, that the real eyes will be opened on the other side of that river, and you will find yourself gazing on trees, but which give no signs of decay, and whose flowers never fade. As I have said before, I see these objects now, so that I need not be moved hence in order to be able to do so. In the meantime you need not these powers of vision, in order to be benefited by a plant or tree. Nor is it absolutely necessary that you should see the plant you are using for your benefit, so long as you know it, either from books or from nature.

The Description of the Psychic Elm, or, how it appears to me on the Soul Plane

In the first place, it is not so massive. Apparently no larger than the Mountain Ash, but as straight as the Poplar. The stem appears free from leaves and branches, all clear for what I should calculate to be ten feet. Then at that point the branches appear in a cluster, and each set of branches spread out in a circular order, each set of branches overlapping the other, so that the top branches of all appear quite flat, and the whole presents the appearance of the top part of a Fir tree inverted, the apex being connected with the stem. The circles of branches are not close together, but appear several inches apart, so that the bloom hangs in bunches like pendants, brilliantly golden, coming down very near the branches beneath; the leaves and bloom appearing, as to shape, very like those of the earthly Elm. There appears about the entire tree a halo, or nimbus, of deep purple, standing out about a foot from the tree, but following its form in all its ramifications. Such is the Elm as seen by me on the soul plane.

The Healing Virtues of the Elm Tree.

The complaints for which this tree is adapted, or to which it applies are: First, the degeneration of the Brain and Nerve matter generally. The symptoms are: extreme languor, and a constant sense of prostration; it usually or sometimes passes for softening of the brain. The person so afflicted suffers no pain, but finally dies from mere prostration. Medical men can do nothing in such a case, nor is there any drug that can stay the progress of this complaint.

I will diagnose this brain matter in its diseased condition, for the benefit of all who choose to read this book. There is a gradual expansion of the brain and nerve matter, which implies a less consistency of the molecular matter of the brain and nerves generally. The more this matter expands, the more it becomes disorganised, and hence less capable of generating and conducting that strange and subtle force, called life force, to the extremities of the body.

Writers when alluding to this subject, appear to convey the idea to me, that each wave of sensation passes direct from the part affected to the brain, which is the supposed organ of consciousness, where all is interpreted, and that the brain being the "house of the Interpreter," gives each sensation its meaning, in such a mode that it becomes the subject of consciousness. But I do not perceive this matter in this light. I view the nerve matter in its ramifications, not only as being the conductor of vital force, but as being a factor of this vital force, so that the whole of the nervous system, if in a healthy condition, is equally charged in every part, so that any local sensation is realised at once, and that without any perceptible interval. But when the molecular particles lose their right consistency, the sensations become intermittent, fluctuating between extremes, until finally such sensations cease altogether.

My next point of enquiry is, what is the cause, or at least the proximate cause, of this break up? I give you what I perceive, and it is possible that science may be able to corroborate these my statements, if so, then will it be the more satisfactory to me. The Nerve matter of such as I have been describing, appears to be granulated with infinitesimal capsules, globular, and as clear as a crystal. These granules, capsules or globules, appear to me to contain water, or a liquid of like transparency. I cannot say if these globules enlarge, or if they multiply, but I am inclined to believe they multiply rather than enlarge, until the consistency of the brain, or nerve matter be broken up, when the life forces cease their circulation. It may not be possible at the present stage of scientific research, to procure a microscope of sufficient power to discover these crystalline globules, in the meantime, it is quite possible that what I here relate may be already familiar to some portion of the scientific world. This fact will not in the least diminish the merit of this revelation, as I have never received a hint from any scientific source relating to the subject; rather would such tend to corroborate the truth of these revelations.

I shall, in the next place, pay some attention to the discovery of the cause of this strange malady. Whatever tends to disturb the equilibrium of the molecular matter of brain and nerves continuously, for any length of time, tends towards the generation of these crystalline globules, or granular formations. When the mind becomes morbidly excited through the undue action of any one function of the body, and that continuously, the normal action of the vital forces is intercepted, and such interception produces an unnatural friction, and this friction becomes a perverted creative force. If a person lives too intensely in the sphere of the imagination; or, if he broods too long over a real, or supposed grievance, or too assiduously or intently devotes the energies of the mind to one special object within the sphere of this every day life; if a person becomes morbidly indulgent towards the gratification of any one of the passions, so as to become a slave to that passion, he then becomes abnormal, and his vital forces run to waste.

I will try once more to make this matter as plain as it may be possible by the use of such words as I may have at command. The life force is a creative force, so long as we live a natural life, that is, so long as the life force passes to and fro in the body, and through the body by way of those ten thousand channels called the nervous system; so long as the molecular particles of the brain and nerves are polarized, so long the life force creates or adds to the nerve matter, replenishes every part of the body with those necessary repairs, which the ordinary wear and tear of every day renders life necessary. But, the moment you settle down to live an unnatural life, by pursuing any of those courses already named, from that moment those life forces become perverted; the brain and nerve matter become depolarized, and the creative force, which should replenish that waste which is natural, becomes perverted, and instead of creating what might add life unto life, it creates, but, what is adding death unto death.

Some grand Intelligence informs me, that a little over one third of the male population of Europe, between the ages of 26 and 45, are more or less afflicted on these lines, and, as a consequence, these will all die before the age of fifty. The proportion of the female population is a little under this amount. These symptoms do not become fixed in the life of a man until his 26th year, after that period the life becomes, in one way or other, a wreck. There is a gradual break up, the process proceeds slowly and almost imperceptibly, nevertheless certainly.

In the face of this gigantic blight, I present mankind with a remedy; a God-revealed remedy; an expenseless remedy; a safe remedy; a universal remedy. You may know what kind of an object the common Elm is. If you have a tree of the kind near you, look at it, contemplate it, admire it until you become enamoured with it. Look at this sigil, and in the absence of the tree, think of it. Go over the Invocation three times or more daily. Every man who works hard with his brain should apply this remedy. The tree takes to itself, or on itself the false formations, and, at the same time, restores to you that lost tranquillity.

This is the sigil
of the
Elm Tree.

The word for invocation
is

The Invocation of the Elm Tree
Ov–al–ack–bah, God of love,
Give thy blessing from above.
Feed my body and my soul,
Ov–al–ack–bah, make me whole.
Out of Thy grand mystery,
Manifested through this tree,
Life renewed to me is given,
Ov–al–ack–bah: life from heaven.

THE BOX TREE
(Bux'us Sempervi'rens)

THIS SHRUB OR TREE IS A MEMBER OF THE SPURGE FAMILY, ONE OF THE MOST NUMEROUS AND DIVERSIFIED OF ANY OF THE FAMILIES KNOWN OR RECOGNISED BY BOTANISTS, IT IS SAID TO EXTEND TO 1500 SPECIES. THE BOX GROUP EMBRACES TREES OF 25 FEET IN HEIGHT, AND TO HAVE AN AVERAGE DIAMETER OF FROM 9 TO 12 inches; such are the Box trees of Turkey, Greece and Circassia. The Box tree of Britain seldom attains to a greater height than from 10 to 12 feet, and down as low as the small shrub of 2 feet, and the yet humbler so-called Dwarf Box, which is used to form borders for gardens and shrubberies, yet under every form or size, and beneath every climate, the Box tree is the same in all its properties. This tree belongs to a poisonous family, and is itself poisonous if taken inwardly in large quantities, at the same time I have known the roots to be used in small quantities with the red dock root as a remedy for Scrofula, and I have known this decoction to effect a cure. The proportion of the box root to the dock should be, to four ounces of the dried dock add one ounce of the small roots of the box. An overdose of box will salivate so as to loosen the teeth.

There are strange and magical properties ascribed to this tree, one of these I here relate: When I was a boy it was customary for men to go about on Easter Monday in gangs, all dressed in their best, and when they entered a house, if the ladies were unsuspecting, they became the easy victims of these amorous marauders, and quickly found themselves placed on a chair and raised up from the floor as high as these knights of cupid could raise them. What they claimed in return was a kiss all round, or if this ordeal was very objectionable, money was given as a ransom to escape from the grip of their captors. We small boys had a substitute for this, we went about from house to house, with a small branch of Box tree concealed under our arms, and on entering the house we set to whipping the lower part of the ladies' dresses opposite the lower limbs. This whipping was supposed to ensure to the married ladies the fidelity of their husbands, and to the young ladies, success in all love matters during the year. Possibly this whipping with the Box may not have a record in any other locality. This custom must have had an origin, also the lifting as it was on the same day. Lest I should weary my readers with what may be considered at this date but a superstitious folly, I will pass on to a description of the remarkable features of the Box tree on the soul plane.

On that plane of light where darkness is not known, this plant appears as a shrub; the branches all at the top and drooping over very much.

The whole plant appears of a deep cream colour, or pale golden, the foliage and stem are also of this delightful hue.

To us, while denizens of this sublunary sphere, the thought of meeting again with those scenes of loveliness and beauty, such as those dear old and familiar shades, beneath the Oak, and other spacious trees, where childhood's playful hours were spent, and sunny youth did laugh and sing; for us to meet again those plants and trees divine, amid those rural scenes where all is sweet, where the plants and trees for ever breathe out their fragrance which we shall continuously imbibe, by which strange process the bodies of "the pure in heart" shall ever live, and being immortal shall plainer and more clearly see their God, must be a source of happiness and comfort.

The complaint for which the Box tree is the psychic cure, has the following symptoms: Acute constrictive pain about the breast bone, attended with anxiety, difficulty of breathing, and a sense of suffocation. Those afflicted with this disease are often seized, when walking up hill or soon after eating, with a painful and disagreeable sensation in the breast which seems as if it would extinguish life. This pain is generally more inclined to the left side of the breast, but does not often disturb the pulse. The pain generally stops quite suddenly when the patient is quiet. The cause very often lies in some positive disease in the structure of the heart, or in the large blood vessels; but sometimes it is only a spasmodic affection arising from imperfect digestion.

This complaint rarely afflicts persons till they have passed their 40th year. The Box tree also fortifies the lungs, and takes away all influences which tend to debilitate the chest, and all complaints of the chest arising from bad, or impure blood.

This is the sigil   The word for
of the   invocation is
Box Tree.   AD-RU-EL.

> AD-RU-EL. Thou God of power!
> Help me in this trying hour,
> Thou who still'st the raging main,
> Liberate me from this pain.
> Through this medium sent by Thee,
> Called by us the Box Tree.
> Awake O God! This pain now quell,
> I Thee invoke, O AD-RU-EL!

THE HOLLY TREE
(I'lex Aquifolium)

I FEEL SURE THAT MY READERS WOULD CONSIDER ANY ATTEMPT ON MY PART TO DESCRIBE A TREE SO WELL-KNOWN AS UNNECESSARY. THE FAMILY OF THE HOLLY IS A SMALL ONE, AND CONTAINS BUT FEW SPECIES. — "THE SPECIES OF THE HOLLY ARE NATIVES PRINCIPALLY OF NORTH AND SOUTH America, the West Indies, and the Cape of Good Hope, and include a good many plants useful to man, the most celebrated being the shrub that yields the Paraguay tea extensively used as a beverage in Brazil and the adjoining governments. A few species from the Cape of Good Hope are esteemed for their foliage, and Prinos from North America are occasional inmates of gardens, but the only one generally cared for is the common European Holly. The tall and sturdy figure; the symmetrically conical form; the glossy and perennial foliage, with the fine effects produced by the innumerable leaves; and the gay bracelets of scarlet berries with which its branches are encircled all through the winter, may well have given pre-eminence to this beautiful tree as well as rendered it the most popular of British plants." — *British and Garden Botany*, by Leo Grindon.

My sympathetic readings within the sphere of the Holly embolden me to pronounce that the Holly is an offspring of the Solar Rays, or, as Astrology would denominate it, a plant of the Sun. It is for this occult reason that from time immemorial its branches have been used to decorate the homes of the people at Christmas-tide. It is about this time that the Sun enters Capricorn, which is that ascending point when the Sun begins to climb out of the darkness of winter, when the days begin to lengthen, and when it may be truly said the Sun is borne, hence it has always been a season attended with hilarity and mirth. This was the custom of mankind long centuries before the advent of Jesus into this world. Some of the early Fathers of the church, when the true Christianity had become corrupted, in order to adapt their religion to the so-called heathen, adopted their festivals, more especially Christmas and Easter, and gave it out that the former memorialized the birth of the Son of God and the latter was in commemoration of His crucifixion which is the time of the Sun's ingress into the Equinoctial sign Aries, when the lord of day is on the cross! such is at that time his position in the heavens. But the true religion of the gospel of Jesus Christ has nothing to do with any of these festivals, they are innovations brought about by the apostasy. There is no command in the New Testament to keep the Sabbath day, and much less is there any injunction to keep a Christmas day. If you chose to keep up that season for festivities and mirth, do so, but not as a Christian rite, for it is a slander on the Christian institution.

The Holly on the Soul Plane

I have not as yet discovered a plant or tree whose identity is so conspicuously manifest on the soul plane as the Holly. It bears a striking resemblance to its earthly type, the only difference being, that where the berries are in the earthly type, from thence proceed tiny jets of golden light of starlike shape, the centres being of fiery red, which conveys the idea of a glow of heat; like so many outlets from one fountain of Celestial Fire which occultly permeates the more inner portions of this wondrous tree.

The Holly applies sympathetically to a greater number of ailments than any other tree I have yet described. It is also generally fortunate, and particularly so if planted on the south side of the house, and more especially is this so if the inhabitant be in sympathy with this tree. This may readily be discovered by attending to the following remarks: The holly is solar in a primary degree, consequently, solar people would derive a benefit through this tree being on the south side of the house. This tree applies favourably to all persons and things under Mars, because when the Sun enters Capricorn, he enters the exaltation of Mars. In such a case the Holly should be on the west side, as this is the position for Mars people and Mars work. It applies favourably to all under Saturn, as Capricorn is the house of Saturn. All persons born under Saturn may derive benefit from the Holly, and should have it placed on the east side of the house. Thus there are three classes of people who are specially benefited by the Holly:– Sun, Mars, and Saturn. The other planetary people may derive a benefit indirectly, that is, through the agency of others, but not directly. This is a point which any Astrologer may discover.

The Psychic Cure

The complaints for which the Holly is the antidote are as follows: Great heat in the throat; constrictive or cramp-like feeling about the region of the heart; spinal affections; virulent pains in the head, accompanied with great heat; parched tongue; intermittent fevers; and delirium tremens.

The secret of all such cases as I have pointed out being curable by the Holly, is this: that element which is the cause of such complaints, is out of its place in the human body, but it is in its place in the Holly. By you thinking about the Holly you become in sympathy with it, and the Holly being negative to that element which is the cause of your suffering, attracts this element to itself, as this is needed by the Holly. It is thus that every plant and tree that grows on the face of this earth absorbs some one element, which by its multiplication out of its own species, generates some characteristic complaint in animal life, which its own species, if sufficiently numerous, would attract spontaneously, but which is often absent from the place where it is required. This defect may be met by the mind directing its energies to that plant or tree independent of position.

Teach this to your children, and who discovered this divine method of cure. It is the duty of all to publish these principles broadcast; seek to instruct your friends, there is nothing to be ashamed of, and you will greatly benefit yourself by so doing. "He who watereth shall he watered."

This is the sigil of the Holly.

The word for invocation is ISH—MAR—ATHEL.

ISH—MAR—ATHEL: god of fire!
Heavenward, upward, higher, higher,
Does thy flame of love inspire.
Consume thy foes beneath thy ire.

THE IVY
(He'dera He'lix)

THE BOTANICAL NAME FOR THIS FAMILY IS ARALIACEÆ. IT IS POSSIBLY THE BEST GENERALLY KNOWN MEMBER OF THE VEGETABLE KINGDOM. IT MAY BE MET WITH EVERYWHERE, EVEN IN PARTS OF OUR LARGE TOWNS AND CROWDED CITIES, ATTACHED TO THE FRETTED WALLS OF ANTIQUE dwellings. The ivy belongs to our much cherished and dearly beloved Evergreens, and will compare favourably for loveliness, with the more exalted species, under favourable conditions, and where the growth is profuse. It is affirmed by Botanists, that there are about 150 different species of Ivy scattered over the earth; but it is with the common Ivy I have to deal in the present article, as this is the plant which contains the greater number of occult properties.

The Ivy held a very prominent place among the ancient Greeks on festive occasions; but especially in the celebration of the feast of Bacchus.

Bacchus is designated the god of wine, and the son of Jupiter. Jupiter, rightly interpreted, signifies Young Father — Ju-pater. This god has ever held the position of 'Father of the gods,' hence he is called "good Father, or, god-father." Notwithstanding all, he had a lewd and drunken son in the person of Bacchus. It is even so among the denizens of earth, many a good father has a drunken son. The feast of Bacchus was celebrated in the Autumn, when the grapes had been gathered, or during the vintage.

It was on these occasions that rejoicings of the most boisterous character were exhibited, and when excesses the most degrading were indulged in amid the shouts of the mad and drunken crowd. It was on such occasions that crowns were worn on the heads of these drunken worshippers. These crowns were composed of Ivy, intertwined with vine leaves.

There is a hidden, or occult meaning in this combination. Whilst on the one hand, the fruit of the vine, which was the cause of that mirth and hilarity was symbolised by the vine leaves; the Ivy, on the other hand, symbolises Sobriety, Durability, Wisdom, and Immortality.

The old Astrologers do assign the Ivy to the planet Jupiter. I will therefore call this plant another son of Jupiter. Such being the case, the Bacchanalian crown represented the two sons of Jupiter.

Hence the Vine and the Ivy represent two brothers of very different characters, it must be confessed. The Vine represents hilarity and mirth, or, what panders to the lower delights. The Ivy, on the other hand represents, or rather symbolises, wisdom and the higher aspirations. Thus it follows, that whilst the Father of the gods gives through his one son all the good things, and even the luxuries of the present life, He, as Father of the Kissos of the Greeks, (the Ivy), stands as the veritable symbol of wisdom, the aspirational, and the spiritual.

The Ivy may be found on any old hedge-cop, in rural districts. Where there is no tree adjoining, to which it may cling with its tenacious holdfasts, it will resign itself to its lowly bed, and become a bush having the fully developed leaves with both bloom and berry. I have witnessed these developments in shady places, and congenial spots in Wales.

But, should there be a tree within reach, it will make use of it in order to raise itself so as to get into a purer air, and also that it may become a partaker of a little more of that light which the trees of the field enjoy. The Ivy appears to be conscious, so to speak, of its own weakness: it cannot stand erect without a support, it cannot raise itself by its own stem. But, when it comes in contact with a tree it will begin to make love to it. It is not particular as to the object of its choice. It matters not what kind of tree; it may be a dumpy tree or a stately tree; it may be a big tree or a small one; it may be a rough tree or a smooth one;

it is all the same, anyone will do for its selfish purpose. The tree in its turn does not appear to appreciate the embraces of the Ivy. I fancy it to say: "O you wretched crawler! You low life thing, how you hurt me. How you disfigure my stately trunk. If you keep on you will hide me altogether from the admiring gaze of my numerous friends." "But," says the Ivy, "I do not rob you of your sap, I supply my own wants from my own roots, I do but make use of your strength so that I may gain a little more of that light, air, and sunshine which your upper branches bask in and enjoy." And thus the Ivy clambers up that sturdy trunk, and envelops the stately stem within its never-relaxing grip, within whose folds the tree pines and frets through hopeless centuries.

This picture which I present you, or otherwise bring under your notice, affords two important lessons: In one light the picture is that of downright selfishness. There are those among the human race whose specious friendship is worse than their open enmity. These make use of the subject of their caresses, merely that they may promote their own selfish ends. Their sole motive, whilst appearing to serve you, how they may elevate themselves, and that at the expense of their confidential friends.

It is thus that whilst they pretend to love you, and to be seeking your interest, they are but making themselves the more conspicuous, until they overshadow you, whilst pretentiously working on their own resources. It is in this way that a mere crawler in the social or commercial world, who, of himself could never have raised himself into notice, becomes a prominent person, simply by attaching himself to one who holds a position in the world, and who is financially stronger than himself.

But, there is another light in which this picture may be seen. The Ivy is the symbol of Wisdom, Immortality, and the higher life. As such it teaches us to look on all sublunary things as subordinate to that higher life. Hence, the Ivy will make use of even the noble Oak in order that it may clamber into the higher, and purer light. Even so are the spiritually minded, those who are imbued with the Divinely aspirational, justified in making the most valuable, the most precious of this world's treasures subservient, or instrumental, towards their spiritual elevation into the light of God. Whilst here on this earth plane there are laws pertaining to this earth life, by which we have to regulate our lives. Whilst confined to this body we have bodily wants which must be attended to, and that we may live at peace with all men, this conventional world has its obligations which we may not forego, but which we are in duty bound to discharge.

I have already suggested that the Vine and the Ivy are brothers; and, I may here offer an additional remark, that there is a wonderful and striking likeness between them. The difference consists in this: the leaves of the Vine perish annually, whereas those of the Ivy are evergreen, or at least perennial, as in fact there is no one leaf, on any one tree, this side *Nirvana* that retains its viridity for years, much less for ever. Each leaf falls in its turn, but it leaves a successor who reigns in its stead.

The Ivy on the Soul Plane

Here it is that its leaf never withers. I am a little doubtful as to whether you do after all retain anything like a true conception as to what is really implied by the phrase "soul plane." Now when I say I see a plant on the soul plane, it must be understood that what I thus see from my present standpoint is an ideal, and has an ideal existence. It is in this light I desire these descriptions to be understood.

By way of further explaining myself, the whole of the visible universe exists, in its true sense, but as a shadow. The real substance is what mankind are in the habit of designating the "unseen."

An Apostle once made the remark, that he — in conjunction with others of like faith — "looked not at the things that are seen, but at the things that are not seen, for the things that are seen are temporal, but the things that are not seen are eternal."

The "not seen" are the ideal, and these are imperishable. The ideal are projections from the Infinite mind, primarily considered. But, secondarily considered, are the ideas of those countless millions of agencies, who work by eternal, and immutable laws. To use but a meagre illustration: The Architect had the plan or specification in his office before a stone of the palace was laid one on the other. There is not an item in the superstructure which had not a prior existence in the mind of the Architect; and, were the whole of that building to perish subsequently, by storm, by flood, or by fire, the ideal would prove to be indestructible.

The idea may have been projected on parchment, or paper, with every specification in detail. This may be reproduced a facsimile of the one destroyed. It is even so with creation. Should this globe, this citadel of man, be destroyed, or become a wreck through the agency of some dread cataclysm, it yet exists, in the ideal within the realm of soul; yes, the ideal survives 'the wreck of matter and the crush of worlds.' This ideal universe has been projected by the Grand Architect, on that spacious canvas called by me the soul world. Every idea is there; the past is there; the future is foreshadowed there; and the Seer or Prophet who may be Divinely inspired can see on that fiery tablet the imperishable Archetype! It is on these same lines that every plant or tree exists for ever in the ideal, and it is by virtue of this celestial existence that the terrestrial plant lives and blooms on the earth. The Ivy as perceived by me on the soul plane, is that of a plant which much resembles its earth type; with this difference: the psychic plant raises itself spirally, each round resting on the one beneath, ascending to a height of what appears to be from ten to twelve feet; thus having the semblance of the trunk of a tree. The top is bushy, and is covered with a white bloom the size of a rose.

The infirmities for which the Ivy is specially, and pathologically applicable, are the following: First, an over-excited brain; the subject of hallucination. Secondly, Sleeplessness, from over-excitement. Thirdly, its moral influence; it begets patience, and resolution. Fourthly, your dreams will prove prophetic.

This is the sigil of the Ivy

The word for invocation is AM–PHRE–NO–MEL!

AM—PHRE—NO—MEL! Thy beautiful green,

Thou picture of love in her emerald sheen.

Take thou the cause of this frailty from me,

It will help thee to climb up a wall or a tree.

Amphrenomel! thou god of the blind,

Comfort my heart, and enlighten my mind.

Amid the dark watches asleep on my bed,

When thoughts most phantastic do tennent my head.

Give me thy light, afford me some gleams,

Preserve me from evil, inspire thou my dreams.

THE COMMON HEATHER
(*Calluna Vulgaris*)

THIS SPECIES OF THE HEATHER FAMILY IS PARTIAL TO MOUNTAIN SIDES. THERE ARE THOUSANDS OF ACRES OF THIS PLANT ON THE MOUNTAINS OF SCOTLAND AND WALES. IT ABOUNDS ON MOORS AND BARREN PLACES WHERE LESS HARDY shrubs do not appear capable of living. This species loves places which are more especially exposed to the sun; at the same time they are capable of enduring any amount of cold, nor does the most severe winterly weather appear to affect their growth.

This may be owing to the presence of essential oil which abounds in the bark and leaves. This may be proved by putting a bush of the Heather on the fire, it will readily ignite and burn fiercely.

There are a great number of species belonging to this family, and, there are some of those species as unlike the common Heather as it may be possible to imagine. I will name a few of those species which Botanists ascribe to the Heather family. The Rhododendron, which may be said to bear no resemblance to the Heather, if examined by a novice in Botany. The Rhododendron is a native of America. It does not grow in a wild state in this country, but is preserved in gardens and shrubberies. The Kalmias is a garden plant, and is also a native of America. The Azalea is a garden plant, and is a native of Asia Minor.

The Strawberry tree (*Arbutus Unedo*), which grows from six to thirty feet, and yields a berry that is good for food. This plant grows abundantly about the Lakes of Killarney. On the rocky Island, Innisfallen, and Bantry. Each of these species belong to the Heather family. It appears, however, that the home of the true Heather is the Cape of Good Hope, which is said to own about 450 different species; how many more abound, both in the eastern and western hemispheres, I am not prepared to say.

I need not go to further lengths with the varieties of species, as each has a genius of its own, and properties of its own. I shall, for the present, confine myself to the common Heather.

This plant is familiar to every one. The purple clothed mountains of picturesque Scotland, which a number of my readers are familiar with, and must have seen. The bloom of this plant is generally profuse. There is but one form of vegetable life in this country, that yields more honey, and that is the red clover. I have somewhere read, that one acre of red clover is capable of yielding one hundred pounds of honey; and the Heather about eighty pounds to the acre. One of the physical properties of this plant is, it is an astringent. It is bitter, but not poisonous, as grouse do feed on its seed, and tender shoots; hence the "land of brown heath," is the land where grouse do abound. I have seen scores of these birds rising out of the Heather when crossing Berwen mountain in North Wales. It has not been my privilege to have read what Medical Botanists may have written as to the properties of this plant, but, I will furnish you with what I get inspirationally as to the medical properties of this humble shrub as applied to the body, outwardly in the form of decoction, or inwardly in the form of tincture.

This plant is, more especially, a plant of the Sun, and, the more its situation is exposed to the Sun, the stronger are its medicinal virtues. Persons of cold and phlegmatic habits, who are liable to inordinate discharges from the bladder or intestines; all such as experience numbness in the limbs, but more especially the extremities, (which are some of the symptoms of paralysis), for such symptoms this is the antidote.

Prepare the tincture as follows: take one ounce of the tenderest shoots, or buds, and pound it in a mortar. Put the well-bruised plant to steep in half a pint of brandy. Allow it to stand in a jar for seven days. Press the whole through muslin. Put a little cold water on the refuse and press it into the prime liquid. Afterwards filter the whole through white blotting paper; bottle it; you have here a valuable tincture. The dose of this is two teaspoonfuls twice a day in milk, or some bland fluid. For paralysed limbs, boil the plant, and make a strong decoction, and apply the same hot, down the spine, with flannels.

In cases of slow action of the heart the decoction applied with flannels out of the hot liquid. This tincture and decoction must not be applied in inflammatory complaints.

When I look at this plant on the soul plane, its glories are bewildering, and its virtues are multiplied, seemingly, a hundredfold. The soul plane of the Heather appears to envelope its earth plane form.

There is a magic in the scene that presents itself. Shakespeare appears to have been the subject of a strange and wonderful inspiration at times.

It was on a heather scene in Scotland that he realised that memorable vision of Macbeth and Banquo meeting the three witches. On which occasion Banquo exclaims:– "What are these, so wither'd and so wild in their attire; that look not like the inhabitants of the earth, and yet are on't? — Live you? Or are you aught that man may question? You seem to understand me." "By each at once her choppy fingers laying upon her skinny lips":– "You should be women, and yet, your beards forbid me to interpret you are so."

That same mountain or moor yet exists. "But," say you, "the three sisters are not there; surely all this was but imaginary, or one of those creations of an omnipotent genius! this was not a reality."

Be not too sure of that. It may be true that those identical personages may not be seen today on that wild heather scene; the witches are no longer on those mountains or moorlands of heather, for Shakespeare's description is a poetic distortion of facts, which witnessed in their true or native state, surpass all of woman born in loveliness and beauty. These pictures of the Poet in this one of his immortal dramas are coloured to suit the church and times.

The Bard of Avon knew that beings, not of earthly mould presided over the Heather; today he is free, and sees these matters in a clearer light.

I perceive a golden light which, like a sea, floods the whole of Heatherland. This light ascends about a yard from the ground, so that the earthly type appears immersed in a sea of glory! This vast ocean of golden light is the effect of a countless number of genii which belong to the Heather, and which preside, each over its own shrub, and each of these gives out rays of light! so that what, at first sight, appears homogeneous, proves to be, on closer inspection, the light from separate entities blending with each other. Each of these possesses a power which we mortals have never dreamed of.

The psychic virtues of the Heather, or what this plant is capable of imparting psychically: Intrepidity, when in the presence of danger; fearlessness of death; a settled state of mind to one place, purpose or thing, no wandering desires for what may be outside or beyond ones sphere.

General robustness of health of body, &c. These blessings, and many more, are imparted by the genius of each plant, to any one who may be in sympathy with the Heather.

I will here give a revelation, which will prove an advantage to the student, and the general reader, in all future researches:– The genii of special honey producing plants, are, with rare exceptions, friendly to the human race. Hence, those plants which give out the most honey, there the genii are most friendly.

These orders of intelligencies are life unto life to every honestly good man; but death unto death to the liar, the traducer, the sneak, and the scoundrel.

The word by which you may heighten the power and virtue of this plant in your contemplations, is VAM–RU–EL. Repeat this word seven times whilst thinking of the Heather, devotionally.

This is the sigil of the Heather.

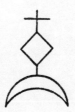

The word for invocation is AM–RU–EL.

The Psychological Properties of Minerals

GOLD

METAL APPEARS TO ME TO CONSTITUTE THE PRIMARY BASE OF ALL MATTER ENTERING INTO THE CONSTITUTION OF THIS GLOBE; AS ALL SOLID, BY THE APPLICATION OF A SUFFICIENT AMOUNT OF HEAT, MAY BE REDUCED TO THEIR PRIMITIVE METALLIC BASE; AS NEARLY ALL THAT IS DESIGNATED EARTHY SUBSTANCES ARE BUT THE OXIDES AND the carbonates of what were metallic solids. There is a substratum, which was at one time supposed to be the true base of all metal, and that is Gold.

As Gold forms the subject of this article I shall seek to throw out such light as my psychic powers may be capable of affording. I am convinced that there is no work published, at this day, that is capable of affording to an inquiring and anxious mind, that information which it needs. I may give this, but I do not make any promise, nor do I enter into any strict engagements relative to this matter, as all such are outside the limits of my own control.

Gold is intimately related to crystal, and is generally mixed up with crystal: so that crystal may be looked on, from a

255

superficial standpoint, as the matrix of Gold. This is its condition in its relation to this crust, which is the third crust from the centre of this earth. The first crust, constituting the primal globe, is pure Gold. Here I do not find Gold allied to any other substance, but so far as my vision will carry me, Gold constitutes the ultimate form of consolidated matter.

Gold may be mixed with other, and inferior metals; but by chemical reagents the true Gold may be detected, and by heat may be brought back to its primitive condition. You have an instance of this in any large china manufactory, where Gold is used for the ornamentation of those vases, jugs, jars, and the familiar cup and saucer. The Gold is placed in a mill, to which is added a quantity of mercury when both are ground up together, the mercury in the meantime kills the Gold, and when this substance is given to the artist it appears but like a bit of blue clay, there is no longer to be found any trace of gold. With this the artist executes his designs on the surface of the unburnt cup or saucer. In this dull condition the design remains until it passes through the baking or burning process; but when it comes from the fire the beautiful Gold appears as fresh as ever, it has parted company with its dirty companion. This is a beautiful illustration of the true and the good in everything. For a time the genuine may be lost from view. But there is always a testing time. Every work shall be tested as by fire, and then the true comes to light; "then shall ye discern" between the truth and the lie; between the wrong and the right. But to return to the primal globe; I have already intimated that within the primal globe exists a light, or brilliancy transcending that of the sun. But this realisation being of a nature so awful, I could not allow myself the temerity that would permit a look within that holy of holies. But I see enough to convince me that Gold is the ultimate in nature; that it, under conditions of which the bookish learned of the schools of science can form no conceptions, constitutes that connecting link between what is called body, and what is designated soul.

In writing on this subject, I feel myself on the outermost boundary line of what may be called effects, which in other words is the phenomenal in its highest state of attenuation! The philosophy I propound is not designed for the amusement of speculative minds but on the contrary, is intended for a purpose, that purpose is to meet and supply some want in human nature. You have a right therefore to anticipate from me something under the present heading that will harmonise with what has been advanced at some lengths on the *Psychology of Botany*.

Minerals are called inorganic matter; that is, matter whose particles are held together by an adhesive force called attraction, but destitute of such parts as point out a distinct being capable of producing certain changes in its own structure, and thereby of affecting certain changes within its surroundings. In the meantime, from the fact that material substances are held together by a force, that force must be superior to those particles which are the subjects of that force; which line of argument goes to prove that there is a soul in everything; and that soul is the secondary cause of every property belonging to that substance. Now, Gold in a sense, is a substance which is the subject of a soul. Adhesion, or attraction is but the manifestation of that soul, pointing out results. But there are connected with this subject heights and depths, which have never been scaled or probed! Gold exists in forms and shapes which mortal eyes have never seen! Gold, in its highest attenuation, becomes fit matter for soul to manipulate, by such an investure it becomes a being having a definite form, and capable of certain operations within its own particular sphere. Such entities are called elements, which I am inclined to consider a very proper denomination for such an order of beings, as the body of such a one consists of a pure element; it is only in such a light that you can define an element, as the body of such a being is not a compound, but is simply the thing itself, and that without alloy. It is possible I may in these remarks be giving in plain terms what has never before been so given.

I now come to deal with this subject in its more immediate relation to the present race. Suffice to say that this race is not, just now, passing through its golden age; nor are there tendencies of such a stature that could afford the faintest hope of such a realisation accruing through any of those recognised agencies now in vogue, and ostensibly for the elevation of the present race.

Each race has one golden age; and seeing such cannot be repeated it might be asked: Why then do you pretend to teach or point out certain principles which may not be possible now, seeing the harvest is past and the summer is ended? My answer is this: that although, as a race, such be impossible, yet there are individual cases where such may be possible.

There are individuals, who, under proper training may yet attain to this enviable pre-eminence; in the meantime knowing what I do of the character of this age, I should not feel disposed to put in a claim for the office of teacher.

Who is there at this day, that moves in such a sphere of quiet and perfect contentment, who would feel disposed to start on a pupilage, amid the labyrinthine mazes of a subject so exclusively transcendental? Do you suppose there is one in a million? There may be, in the meantime, I am not so sanguine as to credit it. My own experience is, that such a person, whilst professing to be my pupil, will in the meantime enter on this state of pupilage charged with notions and opinions; a number of which he considered superior to those of his teacher. All such men, considering themselves my superiors from a world's standpoint, carry this idea into the recesses of their studies. I know that in our universities such is not allowable. The professor of a certain branch is supposed to be superior to his pupil, and the pupil submits to the rules and regulations of the classroom. Not so is the case with me in my experience as a teacher of the occult; hence I view the teaching of such a class as being hopeless in these matters. There are others who manifest a willingness to be instructed; but who are so much the subjects of worry, that their attention is so much divided, that any progress on these lines becomes so intermittent, nothing can be achieved. But the great drawback with all is:– I cannot convince any of the superlative value of such a knowledge. Everything in this day is gauged by a money standard; hence the difficulty which stands in my way of teaching, what I could teach, if the world were otherwise circumstanced. Such a wisdom, in the eyes of the world at this day, is not above that value now placed on "rubies."

The advice I give to thee O man, whoever thou art, and however exalted be thy station in life, is: if thy thirst for Gold be only that of the money-hunter, or the reckless speculator; if thy thoughts go in the general swim in that search for Gold which has now become a craze; yes, a species of madness, then wilt thou perish with the rest who have placed themselves under that terrible curse, which now like a dark pall, hangs over the world; more especially Africa! Has not the reveille been heard already? It is in vain for the newspapers of Europe to cry peace; the elements of destruction abound in the very atmosphere of that fatal land. There are combustibles beyond the ken of mortals; these are destined to explode! Please note this all ye who scoff at prophecy. Africa will ever prove a curse to England! And the present Gold craze will further develop this curse. I have seen this dark cloud over Africa seven years ago. Having made the above remarks by way of digression, I return to my subject. First: what are the occult influences connected with Gold? Secondly: to what kind of people do these influences more directly apply at this day? Thirdly: the special mode of applying these influences. My first remark pertains to those occult influences which accompany pure Gold. These influences in themselves, and when not perverted, are peaceful. Hence, the age of Gold was the age of peace. The Melchizedeckian age was but a remnant of that glorious age; it was but the few scattered rays of the sunset; it was the last flickering light of that departing day which would never more look down upon this fallen race. The Lord Jesus, the Christ of History, belonged to this remnant. He was called a "Priest after the order of Melchizedeck." He came to our world as the last of this race, to bequeath to our fallen race the principles of the golden age; one of the leading characteristics being peace. Hence the song of the Translated Ones on the fields of Bethlehem: "Peace on earth, and glory to God in the highest." Gold in its primal essence is pacific; hence peace and goodwill to all abounded at that blessed period, war and bloodshed was then unknown.

What I am seeking to explain to you I find most difficult, hence the present article will not read so lucidly as I could wish. This is not the communication of some spirit to me, but is the result of my own soul coming in contact with a past time, and experiencing the very feelings which danced through the nervous system, of the men of that day. You will consider some of these remarks extravagant, but I can assure you I do not exaggerate in the least; the fact is, what I state in this book is tame, yes, very tame, in comparison with that reality which I am conscious of. At times I have a sense of smell by which I can realise the odours of plants of foreign climes, such as are unknown to Botanists; not only so, but if you want to know the special medicinal property of all unknown plant, and to what part of the body it may be more specially allied, I could point these matters out. The same holds true with regard to any star or planet situated at any point in the heavens. On these lines my powers have been tested. I refer to these to show that to read those characteristics of the golden age is no more to me than to read the character of a plant or star.

Since Gold has become an article of merchandise those otherwise saving influences have become perverted. What was originally a savour of life unto life has become a savour of death unto death. What was once holy is now prostituted, hence so far as this race is concerned, I may exclaim with the Prophet: "How is the Gold become dim! How is the most fine Gold changed!" The next primal property of Gold is: it gives health and prolongs life. In that celestial period men came in contact with this primal essence, by which their outward nature became so saturated, that any disorder was quite impossible. This was, in the true sense, that "refiners fire." It constituted the true base of the phenomenal universe.

To me this appears to resemble an ocean of golden light. This golden light has evolved out of the mystic purple! It is first born of the parent purple, that thick and impenetrable darkness; the home of the infinite! Out of this golden light have evolved countless millions of objective shadows, designated the phenomenal universe. To me, whilst contemplating this primal matter, the whole of what is called matter appears but as so many shadows. This one primal essence appears to me to be the only real thing. To me, the disappearance of the phenomenal universe appears to be quite in keeping with that grand law: The Divine Breathing. When the infinite inspires, the phenomenal disappears! When he expires, all comes again into the realm of the objective! Between these Divine Breathings, millions of ages may supervene. Thus in the golden age it was a matter of spontaneous occurrence for persons to disappear. Thus, what you read concerning adepts of the past becoming invisible, is within the bounds of truth. I tell thee this is not wholly impossible even at this day. I can testify from my own experience that it is dangerous to bring this poor weak nature suddenly into contact with this essence, as it sends the blood with such fearful velocity through the arteries, that it becomes alarming. But by duly modifying this, and cultivating the mind and soul with certain exercises, this may be used with advantage.

Art thou oppressed in thy spirit and drooping?
Art thou troubled and worried with care?
Art thou disheartened and helpless?
Art thou shut up in despair?
    Pure Gold is the light of thy morning,
'Tis the water of life full and free;
'Tis the sun which succeeds the grey dawning,
'Tis the zephyr of heaven unto thee.
Drink deep, and drink freely poor mortal;
This fountain will ne'er become dry;
'Twill help thee to find that grand portal
Which conducts to immortality!

I must now come down for a time from the realm of the possible, and expatiate on the more immediate and practicable. The question which here suggests itself is: What kind of people are those to whom Gold does not apply beneficially? This may be considered a superfluous question; you will readily conclude that there are none but what Gold will benefit in one way or other. I must, however, at the present stage of research discard from my thoughts that idea of Gold looked on as an article of commerce, in which department Gold is held up as being the standard of value, by which wealth is supposed to be estimated. I would have you banish from your mind all such considerations.

I am now dealing with Gold as the one absolutely ordained medium, subsisting between the soul and the phenomenal universe!

I shall, for a while, allow this grand and essential phase of my subject to stand over, whilst dealing with gold in its more familiar state as a metallic substance. Persons of a very sensitive nature, of thin and meagre appearance, and who are extremely excitable; to these Gold is too stimulating, and will very much aggravate their excitability. People of this description could not carry Gold directly attached to their persons without suffering physically, as Gold is the prime conductor of a force, not as yet recognised by the ordinary scientist. You may call this force what you choose, or by what name you please; but bear in mind it is not what is called magnetism, nor is it electricity, it stands above and beyond all these; it is far more subtle, and a thousand times more powerful; the fact is, there are no limits to its potencies, as there is no standard in nature by which its potency might be gauged.

When I say Gold is injurious to the physical nature of excitable persons, I would not be supposed to insinuate that there is any evil property in the Gold, but that the too fragile organism renders such individuals incapable of holding or containing this element.

I know it is possible for an adept to tap this mystic fountain at will, thus to charge his own physical nature to saturation, and that safely, because, in consequence of progressive initiations, he has previously prepared his body for such influxes, but a novice, knowing of such possibilities, and by recklessly opening this fountain, the same would prove certain death.

He who may have had more presumption than wisdom, would run the risk of being injured, and possibly killed, as suddenly as if struck by a bolt from a thunder cloud. Thus, to people of excitable temperament; whose constitution is weak and fragile; even Gold in its metallic condition, applied directly to the body, would prove too stimulating. In the meantime, even these might benefit themselves by the application of Gold under certain modifications as I will here endeavour to explain: Carry not Gold on the neck, nor yet attached to the ears, but only on the fingers. Go not to sleep with those rings on the fingers, but take them off, and place them in a glass of cold water until again required. Observe: Gold to be of any benefit in this way should be pure Gold, there should be no alloy.

The other class for whom Gold is inapplicable, and who should not carry it on any part of their body attached to their person; are gross, or full-blooded persons; as those in whose nature the animal spirit super abounds, will by such a use, give to their lower nature an additional impetus, and thus what may have been in and of itself a blessing, becomes subverted into a curse. By all such, Gold as a bodily ornament: should be avoided.

The persons to whom Gold applies beneficially are, first: those sluggish natures, where the action of the heart is too slow; persons who are adverse to an active life, whom we usually call indolent; those who generally put off till the morrow what should be done today; those who consider it too soon to begin an enterprise, or undertaking, until it be too late. Persons who never appear to be apprehensive of danger until the disaster be on them. These lymphatic temperaments would do well to have Gold attached to their person. The other class are fair individuals who are weakly and who lack the necessary quantity of blood, a complaint of frequency more especially among the young of the female community, to all such Gold might be applied with advantage. The well-known recipe for this form of disease is Iron, but Gold is far superior seeing it applies directly to those higher and primal functions, those functions which connect themselves with the mainsprings of life where the grosser elements cannot reach or apply because unfit for such attenuated assimilations. There is yet another class I would here refer to, where Gold appears to be applicable, which is that in the case of old people of either sex; those who may not be suffering from any organic disease, and who have not been guilty of injuring the tissues of their constitution by debauchery or through any of those acts which are the characteristics of a vicious life; but where there is merely a sinking, the ordinary attendants on accumulated years with their usual burden of cares, and that exclusively.

By these Gold may be applied with advantage, and if used with judgment according to certain occult laws, such applications may prove the means of prolonging such a life and that indefinitely. It may be asked by some one on reading the above remarks: Do you, who take on yourself to give hints as to the existence of such grand secrets, and that ostensibly for my edification, understand what these laws are? And if so can you teach me how to act so as to secure those high advantages already referred to in your teachings? As to the first part of this question: Do I understand these laws? To this my reply is: Yes, in part. If I were to say less than this I should be acting the hypocrite under a sense of a squeamish fear of being considered presumptuous. If I were to say or profess more than this I should be overstepping the bounds of my present knowledge, and thus make myself, somewhat conspicuously, a public liar.

In the meantime I have a particular desire to impress the following on your mind, whoever the reader of these remarks may be: On all those subjects advanced by me in this volume, I practice what I preach; nor are there ideas in this volume but have for their basis my own highest moral conviction of their veracity, apart from that practical acquaintance obtained in my daily avocations. Hence, if you should find one subject which may not harmonise with your present experiences, you may depend on it the defect lies in your own condition of mind. There must be something that you have not yet discovered in yourself, or taken into account. You may have preconceptions which stand in the way and prevent you receiving what is here offered you, and which acts prejudicially on your mental condition. When such is the case it would be wise on your part to subject yourself to a rigid course of self examination.

I will now attempt to deal with the present subject under its more important, yes I would say, its most important phase, and that from a more clearly defined standpoint. This is: how best to utilise our present relationship to Gold, so as to derive through its mediumship those transcendent virtues; virtues which at this day surpass the highest conceptions of your brightest specimens of worldly wise men, much more the mental grasp of your sordid money-grabbers; by them Gold is enslaved, yes, prostituted.

Note: In the first place the precious metal is wrenched ruthlessly from its most secret of hiding places, where, in the majority of instances, it has laid concealed during countless millenniums! When first found it is so much mixed up with other and grosser matter, that it is only after many serious risks, and sometimes sad adventures that it can be procured. I ask the question: Why is this so? How is this to be accounted for? If Gold was ever intended to become the common drudge of the avaricious, or the plaything of the man of the world, do you not suppose it would have been more accessible? I know of no necessary commodity pertaining to this every day life, so carefully locked up in the conservatories of nature as Gold. It is true you have to mine for coal, but coal after all is plentifully distributed; I think I may say there are few localities destitute of this most valuable combustible. Lead, which is in no sense so indispensable as coal, abounds in great abundance in the hills and mountains of my native country, Wales. Tin may also be procured in sufficient quantities to meet the requirements of the household. The same may be said of other useful and serviceable metals, but Gold, considering its vast circulation, as a coin of the realm, and for ornamentation, is exceptional. The fact of the matter is: Gold was never intended by the Creator of the universe to be degraded to an article of merchandise, or the standard of representative value. Gold as seen by me on the psychic plane, is not in its place when in the hands of the money changers; it is a power for good in its proper sphere, hence, having become a perverted power, it has entailed on the present race a heavier curse than all and everything besides.

The error of the old Alchemists consisted in fostering avaricious designs by which the majority of them were actuated. At the same time, some few of these men had much higher aims than to add so much bullion to the national exchequer. A few of these most venerable sages had found the "Philosopher's Stone," they had proved to their own satisfaction that the elixir of life was something more than a dream. These men never coveted Gold in its metallic form so as to enrich themselves after the fashion of the men of the world. These sages had scaled the rugged hill of difficulty; they had attained altitudes so as to be able to look down with a feeling akin to a holy and righteous contempt on the Gold hunters of the world. Thus, to be able to derive from Gold those occult benefits it is capable of affording, you must, in the first place, overcome that feeling of covetousness for its accumulation as a possession or a property, and that in excess of what may be absolutely demanded from you for the present necessaries of life. It is quite true, that as society is now organised, and as now governed constitutionally and commercially, we are obliged to have in our possession this "coin of the realm;" and since one pound sterling is supposed to represent that amount of time and labour expended on the article we purchase at such a valuation; we are thus compelled to present this equivalent before we can become the possessor of the article we need. Could I procure the necessaries of life without this currency, I can safely say that I should feel no ambition to become the possessor of money for its own sake, or as a mere toy, in which light it is estimated by thousands. The happiest moments of my life have been those, when implicit confidence has taken such a hold of my soul that I could triumph over every doubt, having this assurance: "Thy bread shall be given thee, and thy water is sure." Let it be distinctly understood, that the coining of Gold into money, and thus placing it in the general currency, is a dishonour to that article; and whatever tends to augment this currency, tends to curse this world with every kind of vice; including war rapine and every form of cruelty.

To give Gold the honoured place of ornament is right, so long as such ornamentation arises from the love of that inherent beauty which pure Gold possesses. Gold thus used will bring a blessing. So far as my own feelings are concerned, I possess a love for Gold which approaches reverence; a reverence which some may suspect as bordering on superstition. But knowing what I do of this grand element; (excuse this term as I view it in this light;) when I see it in a befitting condition, where all within its surroundings are worthy of such an ornament, then, and only under such circumstances do I recognise Gold as in its proper place. In that reckless use of Gold as personal ornament in the form of rings or chains, if not worn from the purest and loftiest of motives I say it would be far better you did not carry such on your person at all. But if your whole soul be open to receive the highest influences; and should you feel a love for Gold as being the metallic medium for the spontaneous influx of celestial virtues, from the Solar and the "Geozonic Spheres;" if the pleasure you experience in having on your person golden ornaments be as great in secret, where no mortal eye can see, as in public, or even greater, then, and under such conditions you will be blessed.

The next vice to be conquered is covetousness; not to allow the desire for its accumulation as an article of so much value as estimated by the merchant in the money market. When you, who have in your possession thousands in Gold, look on these valuable articles, say not to yourself these are worth so much, and with these I can purchase so much in such a market and thus add to the stock I possess, and finally by these transactions I shall become rich. Rather say to yourself, I hold in my possession a Talisman, the grandest of all material substances. I will henceforth look on these valuables, not as "Sordid dust," but as the veritable mirror in which I see soul beauties reflected.

These treasures are to me that primal matter, that first vesture in which my living soul enwrapped itself from that eventful moment when God breathed the "Breath of life;" or Life-breath.

Under the auspicious reign of Solomon, Gold appears to have been very abundant; this abundance according to our Bible account, was not recognised by a large circulation as a medium for representative wealth, but more especially by way of ornamentation. Behold the temple at Jerusalem, which was the grandest work of Solomon's reign or since the birth of history. What must have been the amount of Gold then used as ornament within the magic precincts of that stupendous pile! This house was intended to be the centre of an influence; a pivotal point, from whence a power radiated, by virtue of which the whole land of Palestine was blessed. Not only so, but this influence extended to the stellar orbs of heaven. Read that marvellous covenant made with Solomon by a plenipotentiary of Jehovah in the 2nd Book of Chronicles, the 7th chapter. You who thirst for a knowledge of magic on a grand scale, read this account of the temple as a centre of power. Read the 1st Book of Kings, here you will see what a prominence was given to Gold in the building of the temple. Also the quantity, which is an enigma to the learned of this century. Read for yourself. Ask yourself where did all this Gold come from? It is said to have come from Ophir. Ophir is a mountain on the Malay peninsula in the East Indies, near the equator, about 105 degrees East Longitude. This Gold was the result of natural washings, and according to my vision there had been a convulsion of nature by which a quantity of Gold was thrown to the surface, no doubt this was brought about by miraculous power. We have no reason to suppose that the Gold used by Solomon in the decoration of the temple came from any mine.

King Solomon had a navy of ships, these were under the supervision of his grand agent Hiram. Hiram had servants under him who were conversant with navigation, with these he probably sailed direct from the Persian gulf into the Indian ocean, and thence to that mountainous peninsula called Ophir, which is situated about twelve miles from Malacca. See the 9th chapter of the 1st Book of Kings 27th verse. In addition to this, the fame of Solomon had been wafted to every clime. His great wisdom had won for him the good will of every Monarch of the East. These sent him presents of Gold and other things. It is recorded that "All the earth sought to Solomon to hear his wisdom, which God (or the gods) had put into his heart." And each of these potentates brought with them presents of silver, and Gold, and garments, and armour, and spices, and horses, and mules; a rate (or tribute) year by year. Among these grandees we find special mention made of the "Queen of Sheba;" in another place, the "Queen of the South;" and in another place she is said to have come "from the uttermost parts of the earth." That Sheba is now called Abyssinia. This great Queen of Bible renown loaded Solomon with her kindness in presents of all kinds including Gold.

Thus this mighty Sage and King conquered the world without bloodshed. His armies never rendered parents childless or wives widows. No smoking villages or blood-stained battle fields marked his progress to greatness and to glory. His power was on the soul plane. Inspirations from the intelligence of Jupiter, combined with the wisdom of the Angel of the Sun. He had the glorious trine of the sun and Jupiter at his birth! At his birth the sun was in Sagittarius, on the ascendent, and Jupiter was in Leo. Mercury was in Scorpio, which is not an intellectual sign, but psychical. His moon was in the sign Pisces. Thus the mental rulers were in psychical signs, and disposed the whole nature of this great King to become the recipient of such real living wisdom. And it was under the influence and guidance of this most excellent wisdom that Solomon gave to Gold the most prominent place in the most sacred services and rituals of that Magical Fane at Jerusalem.

That temple at Jerusalem may very pointedly symbolise that superior temple: the human body, or the entire human being, consisting of body, soul and spirit: The outer court; the Temple; and the Holy of Holies. Every vessel of that house was pure Gold, even so every power put forth by the soul of man has its base in pure Gold! This elemental Gold is that inner temple which is called the Spiritual body. The Spirit has built up for itself this Spirit body which is called the soul, and by virtue of this inner body the outer body has been formed.

The inner body partakes of the semblance of the Immortal Spirit, and if this inner body continues in unison with the Spirit, which is called the I Am, it will itself become immortal, and will continue to be the temple of the Spirit, or the I Am! But if that soul or inner body revolts; if the psychic powers say we will not have this one to reign over us, it will forfeit its immortality; it then becomes broken up and diffused among its kindred element, and the Spirit returns to its fountain from whence it came, and that personality ceases to be. Consequently, for man to gain immortality he must "work out his own salvation," he

must build up the inner house which is "his house from heaven."
The soul, the Spirit body, has for its base elemental Gold.

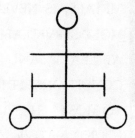

This is the sigil
of Gold.

Bright elemental essence! a little I unfold

Of thee within these pages; but much is left untold.

A residuum remaineth which ever will transcend

These fitful lucid glances:– This temple veil must rend.

This veil of flesh which intercepts; cloud-like it comes
    between

Me and those glowing spaces; thou all absorbing sheen!

Unchanging are thy glories, whilst ages onward roll;

Thou vestibule of God-head! — My soul! — Thou art my
    soul!

ELEMENTAL IRON

THIS METAL, ALTHOUGH NOW ESTEEMED AS BEING ONE OF THE COMMONEST OF METALS, IS NEVERTHELESS, ONE OF THE MOST SERVICEABLE TO MAN IN THIS AGE AT LEAST, AND THAT UNDER PRESENT CONDITIONS. IT IS A FACT WELL-KNOWN TO MOST, THAT IRON IS RARELY, IF EVER, FOUND NATIVE, AS ACCORDING TO ALL MODERN TESTIMONY IT IS ONLY obtainable through a chemical process, from a species of earth or stone called Iron-Ore. Such is the ordinary source, from whence the Iron of commerce is obtained. It is with such Ore I have to deal in the present article; as it is with such primal matter those ideas are allied which will be evolved in the present work. The Iron of commerce is purely an artificial commodity, for as much as it has been brought to its present stage of malleability by the application of art to the purposes of science. It has been said by some authors, that Iron, similar to the Iron of commerce, has been found native in Siberia, and in parts of South America. But whatever may be advanced relative to this matter, we know that so called native Iron must have passed through the smelting process under conditions analogous to what the Iron of commerce has passed through before becoming malleable Iron. This phenomenon may, I think, be rightly classified among meteoric productions.

The purest and best Iron is made from an Ore called Haematite. This Ore is of the same nature as the red corpuscles in the blood, hence it is, there is none other of the metals so essential to animal life. But, before it can be taken up and assimilated by the absorbents it must be reduced to a state of purity by oxidation. This process is easily obtained through exposure to the atmosphere of a portion of the best malleable Iron, when the oxide becomes developed in the form of what is called rust, in which condition it resembles its primitive state from which it has been manufactured. In the meantime my department lies outside, above, and beyond the rigidly scientific, and supersedes the artistic. I shall therefore proceed to note what may be discovered on the soul plane relative to this subject.

In the first place I perceive that the soul force emanating from this sphere of the pure Ore called Haematite is most positive in its nature, and powerful in its operations. Indeed, in some instances, and under conditions relating to the sphere of humanity, unpleasantly so. It must be borne in mind that this applies to Elemental Iron which is met with on the soul plane, and there only. For however pure it may be considered on the material plane, it must of necessity contain a subtle quantity of something that is not itself. This theory extends over the whole domain of matter; there are but few instances, if any, of metallic substances being found pure. But on the soul plane these amalgams are unknown, as each metal exists eternally in its placid homogeneity. This phraseology I am now using, but feebly expresses the idea of that absolute oneness or selfhood I perceive exists on the soul plane. Vainly do scientists dream of such an achievement in their search for the pure elemental part of any one thing on the physical plane, it is only within the realm of soul where such exists in perennial youth and fadeless loveliness. This elemental Iron is not only the most positive, but is also the most attractive to every form of life abounding on this globe, for this reason: It is more nearly allied to the life and love in nature than any other element with which I am yet acquainted. Consequently it necessarily possesses the greater number of those agencies who are connected with the objective universe.

This Haematitic Ore when reduced to its most perfect state as it exists in pure blood, becomes a magnet attracting to itself those tiny agents who in the exuberance of their mirthfulness and glee, send the red corpuscles with a momentum capable of countless evolutions during a period of sixty, seventy, or eighty years. When another influence intervenes, an influence which chills or retards the ordinary rush through those channels of life, then do these small people die, sometimes suddenly, at other times more gradually; but in each case the red corpuscles become vitiated, or the condition becomes changed prior to the departure of these life agents.

Additional to these, there are greater Beings who appear to sustain their relationship with living things by virtue of Elemental Iron. I have made these few remarks which are but mere fractions of what I know, but further communications would be useless.

Those for whom Elemental Iron is more especially applicable are persons of pale or sallow complexion, of a cold nature, and where the blood is deficient in quantity, in the meantime, no organic affection, as the organs of the body must be fairly sound when this force is turned on, as it may come with such a bound into the vital parts of the body, so that a very much deranged organism would be incapable of enduring the shock or strain.

There are possibly as many who die from these sudden inrushes of the life forces, as there are from the lack of these forces. The engine with great steam capacity, requires that the whole of her works should be proportionately strong, if there be any departure from this the result would be a break down, and possibly that may be attended with disaster.

The class of persons who should never take Iron in any of its preparations are the full blooded, and those whose blood may be in an impure condition, such invalids should shun this metal as a medicine. The saline influences of the ocean are best for all such as these. On the other hand, those who are in want of blood should avoid the ocean or seaside resorts, many a life is sacrificed through this species of popular ignorance. I hope these hints may not be given in vain. The word to be used for this metal is: AR–PHO–RI–EL. This word is an invocation and should be repeated seven times.

This is the sigil
of
Iron.

The word for invocation is
AR–PHO–RI–EL.

COPPER

THIS METAL HAS BEEN KNOWN FROM THE FURTHEST ANTIQUITY. ACCORDING TO, EVEN MODERN CALCULATIONS, THE CHINESE WERE FAMILIAR WITH COPPER, AS A CIRCULATING MEDIUM, NEARLY ONE THOUSAND YEARS BEFORE OUR ERA HAD DAWNED; AND WHICH HAS REMAINED SO EVER SINCE, HENCE IT IS, AT THIS DAY, THE STANDARD COIN OF THAT VAST EMPIRE. IT IS TRUE THAT HER MERCHANTS, IN THEIR TRANSACTIONS WITH THE FOREIGNERS, MAKE USE OF SILVER, AND THAT WITHIN CERTAIN LIMITS, CONFINED TO THE TOWNS, where Silver and Gold may have supplanted Copper currency; yet, even at this day, in the rural districts of China, Copper remains the standard representative of value. This metal, like most of the other metals, is seldom procured in a pure condition from the mine; but is rendered pure by a chemical process, but with such processes I am not concerned, as it is with Copper as generally known that I am treating.

In prehistoric times Copper had a value exceeding that of Gold, and occupied a position among the Pythonians like Gold does with us at this day; hence the Chinese, being a relic of the Pythonian race, still hold Copper as being of more real value than Gold. The Chinese are not guided by our civilisation in their policies only when compelled to do so; and when a Chinaman appears to endorse the views and religion of modern civilisation it is but outwardly he does so, and is simply adopted for policy-sake. The Chinese descent is not from the fallen portion of the Pythonian race, but from the line of Adepts; that remnant who preserved their faith, the true faith, amid that corruption which abounded prior to the overthrow, and subsequent extinction of the diabolical portion of that race. These grand ones inhabited Mongolia; that is, the bulk of them; but a few of the more advanced inhabited Palestine.

This great people were designated by a name, which in English has its equivalent in the word celestial. Here we find a reason for the epithet 'Celestial' which the Chinese of today consider themselves entitled to. Hence the Chinaman's pride of ancestry is no vagary. It is for this reason that Copper holds so high a place among them, and still holds its place as the standard coin of the realm.

But there are secrets — at least relatively speaking — connected with this metal, such as were once well known, which are hidden from all eyes at this day. I will in all humility consult those immortal records of celestial wisdom, wherein I find that which defies the probings of the excavators in Assyria, Egypt, or classic Greece to unearth. Be it known to you, wise men of the west, that the man who holds in his possession the key which can unlock those mystic archives of forgotten lore, which ye now search after with pick, shovel and crowbar, is the one you despise, yes, and what is yet worse, ignore: Go on; yes, I say go on! You will never find what you are seeking after; no, never!

You have read of the Stone age; the Copper age; and the Iron age. The Stone age has been set forth in anything but complimentary terms. They are supposed to have been destitute of the knowledge of any of the metallic substances in nature save that of Stone, a substance which I shall call semi-metallic.

This supposition the Antiquarian forms on the following fact: that amid the relics of a pre-historic period no other instruments are found save what are made of Stone. But the men of the Stone age were not ignorant of other metals; only that for reasons which I shall here produce. Among the whole range of substances in nature, there was not one so valuable in their estimation as Stone, more especially the Flint Stone. In the meantime, be it known to all, it was not from a utilitarian point of view that they were guided in forming this estimate; at least not exclusively so. They looked on the Stone as being more directly the property of a god, and as being more the work of his hands. Hence they considered the Stone — the Stone which lay in their path — as having been handled by a god. In the Stone they could see marks, which we would call hieroglyphics, by which they were guided as by an oracle. The everlasting rock they esteemed, as being the work of a builder god; thus being in harmony with a Bible phrase at this day: "whose builder and maker is God." Thus the Stone was most valuable because most sacred. It has ever been the conviction in the past that the more intimate the relationship supposed to exist between any substance in nature and the Great Spirit, the greater was its value. Psychically, the men of the Stone age were far in advance of the men of subsequent ages, or even of this age. These men made many a stupid blunder on the physical plane of life. They were so primitive in their notions of this outer life as to be nearly helpless. The bodily organic intellect was not developed, but the soul was strong and healthy, and full of fire. The God was in that soul, couched, perchance, in some rude form; he was one who heard his God in the thunder; in the stormy wind; in the babbling brook; and who saw Him in the wild and frantic motions of the branches of the forest trees, whilst shaken by the wind "when the trees of the field do clap their hands."

This law of thought may be said to have existed in the estimate which was formed of Copper in the Copper age; at the same time not so implicitly or so completely as in the Stone age.

During the Copper age, this metal was esteemed as being the most valuable of all others, because of the inherent magical virtues which were known to exist in this metal. It was known to possess a strange influence which was designated the Breath of God.

The Stellar influences of this metal are those of Venus in the sign Taurus. Hence, anyone desirous of obtaining such an influence for any specific purpose let him engrave that purpose on Copper, along with the Sigil given, when Venus is in this sign. This grand influence acts as a tonic to the soul; whilst it is the very opposite on the physical plane. Hence Copper is magnetically an antispasmodic; it is clonic which is the opposite of tonic. Thus it is that when Copper is applied outwardly to any rigid limb, it tends to relax that rigidity. But Copper on the soul plane, or when that aura is imbibed by the soul, enriches that soul, by giving it a power which attracts to itself entities that are in sympathy with Love, Wisdom, Wonder, Admiration, and all the higher attributes of the soul.

These attributes will inevitably render that person's nature super-terrestrial, and will tend towards forming conditions for those higher forms of development which will ultimately render that person a companion of the gods; like one of old, who "walked with the gods." He will become a natural Seer; a natural medium; a natural soul philosopher. I am obliged to use words and phrases which may sound harsh. Thus the men of the Copper age were not possessed with that kind of brute courage which is so necessary for battle and carnage. But they were the most courageous on that field where a moral war is waged. They invariably possessed the courage to say No, when asked to do what might be wrong. This is an attribute which is lacking in the warriors of this day. There be many who could face the musketry of the battle field with the aspect of valour and bravery, who could not find the courage to act up to their convictions.

The Copper age men were a people endowed with great moral courage, and they obtained their reward.

I now come to speak of those virtues which belong to Copper, and those uses to which it may be applied by the soul, and on the soul plane.

Copper applies itself to all those persons who may be anxious to speak and to do the right, but who are lacking in the courage to do so; as such an advance would incur the risk of being considered singular, or otherwise eccentric. The really truthful man or woman at this day, is generally looked on as eccentric or a crank. What is most popular, generally speaking, is dependent on what is false for its popularity; and that which is false is a lie. To be truthful is not really considered to be good policy. This idea permeates all the higher branches of state officialism. The most accomplished diplomatists are those who can fabricate the most plausible falsehoods. Thus to tell lies on these high lines has begotten for itself an almost enviable popularity; this spirit pervades every governmental department in Europe. You may, as a private individual, tell any amount of lies, or publish the same through the dailies or weeklies, or in book form, so long as they are uttered in fashionable language, and are kept within the domain of laudation, where eulogistic phrases are the current articles. Some of you may see the force of these statements. Some of you may feel grieved at the present corruption which abounds on these lines. You feel you would like to oppose all this so far as your influences may extend, but you lack the courage to do so; you fear to lift up your voice against all this; you would thereby incur the frowns of some of your friends, some who may not be able to see with you.

I offer you a soul strengthener in the Copper. Look at this Sigil, it symbolises a Power, a Hierarchy, a Government, founded on Truth. The subjects of this government have a helmet, but it is the "Helmet of Salvation." They have a shield, but it is the "Shield of Faith." They have a sword, but it is the "Sword of the Spirit." They are clothed in a complete armour, but it is "the whole armour of the gods." That influence which belongs to Copper is conducive to the establishment of those conditions for the development of that reign of rightness, which is destined to exist for ever and ever. The Name and Invocation: AV–MAH–HU–JAH.

This is the sigil
of the
Copper.

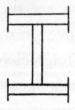

The word for invocation is
AV–MAH–HU–JAH.

O adorable light of the ages!

Thy ways are marked in imperishable characters
in the heavens, and in this earth.

Thy Love, O Matchless One, is that of a mother,
who never forgets her helpless one that hangs
at her breasts for its life.

The mysteries of thy government extend unto
the heavens, and the earth is filled with thy
goodness.

O thou who ridest on yonder celestial
constellation by thy name AV–MAH–HU–JAH!

Clothe me with thine armour; shield me with
thine hand; watch me with thine eye.

Make me strong in thee, and in the power of
thy might.

Amen.

The Psychological Properties of Precious Stones

The Topaz of Ethiopia
shall not equal it.

JOB 28:91

THE TOPAZ

As a matter of change, I am disposed to turn my attention to another department of nature.

The realm of Precious Stones abounds with wonders which transcends everything I may have hitherto been made conversant with. Hence, I am very much fascinated with these lustrous specimens of a chemistry which transcends the skill of the ingenious to identify, or to produce the same. It is true that so far as appearance goes, modern skill can produce from a kind of paste what resembles the genuine Stone, but he can no more produce a living Stone than he can make a living tree.

The true Stone has a life, and it is in this life that its true virtue consists. In this respect the wealthy have advantages which the person of small means has not, as the former can purchase the genuine article, while the latter but too often satisfies his vanity with an imitation. The anti-Occultists may say, in the face of what I am about to say respecting the Topaz, that, chemically considered, it is made up of a proportionate amount of Silicon. Aluminium, and Fluoric acid; and, say you, what wonderful properties may such a well-known compound contain? The same scruple might be raised against the occult virtues which are known to exist in plants or animals, including man himself, as each may be made a subject for chemical analysis, each part looked at separately are but well-known gasses, liquids, with an admixture of common substances, such as lime, iron, with their phosphates, yet mighty forces are made known through this compound.

But say you, the plant or the animal is what we designate "organic matter"; and is it not in consequence of such an organisation that the being proves the medium for such forces.

My reply is this: The word "organic" is to my mind but a comparative term. A Zoophite may be said to be a poorer specimen of organic matter than the Mollusca and so on upward in the scale of animal life; there are species of vegetables that appear to hold but a dubious frontier between the vegetable and the mineral. But all matter which is consolidated in the form of stone or mineral of any kind is organic, and the Topaz is as much a species of organic matter as the Oak of Britain, or the Cedar of Lebanon. It will be my task to explain what may appear to be mystical relative to the Topaz.

I may, in the first place, affirm that but few of the ordinary class of jewellers know how to distinguish the real Topaz from the spurious. I find it described by Dr Graham in his chemistry as being yellow. But the colour of the most valuable species of Topaz is a light pink yellow, that is, a light yellow with a tinge of pink. It approaches the hue of the flesh of an infant, and is transparent. This is the colour that comes before my psychic vision whilst writing; hence, the statement that the Topaz is yellow is false.

This Stone has magical properties, and will effect much in the possession of the right class of persons.

The sort of people to whom this Stone applies, and that beneficially, are the fair people with weak or fragile constitutions, and are inclined to become despondent, and who are withal of cold habits. To such the magic of the Topaz will prove of great service.

There is another type for whom the Topaz may prove helpful; these are of that class who are generally out of sight, or in the shade, not recognised by the more prominent or conspicuous members of society. The nature of its influence is to beget hopefulness in the hopeless; to strengthen and fortify the soul against the fiery darts of the designedly wicked, and wilfully cruel and unjust persons. It partakes of the influence of Jupiter and Venus, with a colouring of Mercury.

Here it may be asked: is there no way of being made a partaker of these influences which belong to, or are derivable from the Topaz, by such individuals as may not be sufficiently opulent to become the actual possessors of the stone itself? My reply is: most certainly it is possible, and that by the use of the Sigil of the Topaz which is the true expression of the Divine idea, and that idea is the genius of the Topaz.

But this idea is too much involved to be uttered or expressed by any syllabical form of utterance; hence it is evolved, or projected outwardly by a figure, or a diagram, which is founded on Geometrical principles, which principles are eternally true and immutable, though a Euclid had never lived; yes, further, though an Angel or a God did not exist.

Truth absolute, is uncreate; it never had a beginning, and therefore it cannot have an end. "Two things equal to the same thing are equal to one another. This is designated an axiomatical truth. In the meantime it has no creator, but it has had many discoveries; for problems innumerable do hang on this, or, do arise out of this Axiom.

This is the sigil
of
Topaz.

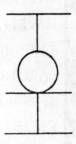

The word for invocation is

SOO—MAH—THU—EL — DI—VOO—MATH—EL.

The next matter of importance is the sacred name: SOO—
MAH—THU—EL — DI—VOO—MATH—EL.

If those who need the virtues of the Topaz, but may not
possess the stone, and to whom such do apply, will make a
practice of the above Invocation, daily at the hour of sunrise;
having the sigil or stone before them, five times, they will attract
to themselves an influence which the conventionally wise of
this world cannot give them; by virtue of which, he or she may
become changed into the Divine Ideal.

THE AMETHYST

THE AMETHYST IS ONE OF THOSE PRECIOUS STONES WHOSE MYSTICAL, OR OCCULT PROPERTIES, HAVE BEEN KNOWN TO PORTIONS OF THE HUMAN RACE FROM THE EARLIEST DAWN OF HISTORY. OF THIS WE HAVE PROOFS IF WE BUT REFER TO A GREEK LEXICON, WHEREIN WE MAKE THE RATHER IMPORTANT DISCOVERY THAT A PRECIOUS STONE IS THERE GIVEN under the name Amethyst, whose virtues are said to be that it is an antidote for drunkenness. *Methu* or *meddu* is the Greek for what we in our language call drunkenness. There is a similar word to this in the Welsh language which applies to the same thing, and which is pronounced very much alike. In former times in this country, and that within my own recollection, they had a species of an intoxicant made from the honeycomb after the honey had been extracted, as some of the honey would certainly adhere to the cells after the bulk of it had been taken out. This was then utilised by immersing the combs in hot water. I recollect this much, as my mother was in the habit of making this species of strong drink when the time came round for the destruction of the bees. The combs were allowed to stand in this hot water for a time, the liquid was fermented with the application of yeast, and this fermented liquor was put in a cask for subsequent use; this liquor we called *meth* or *medd*. This drink was very intoxicating. What I here state is from memory; it is quite possible that this practice may not have yet become extinct, and that the people of the present day may be familiar with this kind of manufactured drink, more especially beekeepers. If such be the case, I have been relating, and that but imperfectly, what is superfluous. But what I wish to make clear is that the earliest intoxicants, or at least one of the earliest, was made from the refuse of the honeycomb, and that this liquor was called *meth* or *medd*, which applies to the same origin as the Greek word *methu*. Hence it follows that *methyst* would belong to the same, and must signify drunkenness. But the letter *a* being a prefix to the Greek noun *methyst* changes the whole character of the noun, as the *a* in Greek has the same signification as our adverb *not*. Thus it follows that the signification of the word Amethyst, translated into English, is *not-drunk* or *no-drunk*.

Under such favourable aspects I should suppose that every temperance man, who may read this article, must of necessity become enamoured with this precious stone, For, although a prevention is said to be better than a cure, at the same time, if a man who is drunk could be restored to his senses by the influence of the Amethyst, and that quickly, I consider that this same influence would destroy or otherwise nullify that peculiar fascination which attends the drinking of intoxicating liquor. Drunkenness must then, of necessity, cease altogether. For the one object that most men have in drinking intoxicants is that they may become drunk! And as incipient drunkenness lies concealed in the very first drop that is admitted within the lips, this peculiar fascination becomes stronger and stronger with every additional draught, until a sober community will consider it no exaggeration in saying that the man, or the woman, is drunk.

I will not presume to say that the Amethyst will do all that is supposed to be claimed for it in this article, and that *directly*. But I dare to say this much: "Wine is a mocker, strong drink is raging, and whosoever is deceived (fascinated) thereby is not wise." The inner sense of the whole of this matter is this: that the very *desire* of an intoxicant, as a beverage, is an indication of a species of incipient insanity. For whatsoever does not harmonise with the laws of our nature (that nature which has been given us by the author of our being) must, be attributable to some other or extraneous force, which promotes transgression of this law, and which is unnatural. This desire for intoxicants springs from the same root as the desire for narcotics.

Forasmuch then, as to the greater majority of mankind intoxicants and narcotics do present a strong fascination towards indulging in the use of these, I am forced to the conclusion that the majority of mankind are suffering from some derangement of the mental or psychical faculties, and that this derangement is no more or less than incipient insanity. I therefore consider it incumbent on everyone to make use of any and every means which may come under notice within the limited range of our information, to cure this deep-seated and long-lived infirmity.

Total abstinence has hitherto been the only means at our disposal by which to combat this great evil. At the same time, total abstinence but simply protects the man or the woman from some of the more terrible results or consequences of drinking and of drunkenness; but this abstinence is incapable of eradicating out of man's nature so deeply-rooted a disorder, one which render mankind the victims of such allurements. I therefore hold that it is here at this important stage where the influence of the Amethyst may be proved to be of incalculable value. I proclaim this from a higher platform than that of merely scientific researches. God, in the order of His providence, has made ample provisions for every real want His creatures may possess, and therefore we may, from a rational point of view, consider it not an improbable matter that the Amethyst may be the specially ordained instrument which is calculated to meet this very sad, grievous, and urgent necessity. In the meantime, I am certain it *is* the very antidote not only for this form of incipient insanity, but for other mental infirmities or hallucinations, such as I shall shortly allude to.

It is quite possible you may look on this stone as being a mere chemical compound, whose primary substance is quartz or crystal, as crystal constitutes the primary basis of the greater part of precious stones or gems. The crystal appears to me at this day, in its primal state, on the lowest stratum of this cosmic crust in that formation which adjoins that circumambient space which lies at the bottom of this crust on which we reside. At this point it is liquid, but of great density; but as there is nothing below but what may be found above, it is so in this case, the only difference being that what is liquid one thousand miles below is solid on and near our surface. At the same time the crystal in its solid form is lighter than what it is in its liquid condition.

I write this in the present tense, as I see or realise what I give in this article. Further, bear this in mind: this earth is not a huge bombshell, charged within with liquid fire. This is one of the greatest delusions ever published, save that which has been said of the Sun, — these popular delusions or falsehoods which I have years ago refuted in my *Geozonic Spheres*. The crystal, whose primary condition is liquid, in its upward gradations, forced by chemical agencies, becomes tinged with the hues of other substances, hence the variegated colours by which the different gems are characterised. The colour of the true and genuine Amethyst is that of a deep, rich, violet blue. The true stone possesses shades within its composition which defies imitation in either glass or paste, but these are very difficult of description.

Having gone to some length in this article in what may be designated preliminary to the subject in hand, at the same time what is really involved in my subject, I proceed to notify those additional disorders for which the Amethyst is the antidote. Should a person have false vision, that is, he is liable to see in the twilight different kinds of forms and shapes, what may be expressed by the generic term, vagaries. For all such cases this stone is the antidote. The next complaint is a degenerating memory, more especially when you want to recall the name of some person, place, or thing. The next is that of colour-blindness.

These disorders or defects in our mental or visual constitution may be benefited, if not cured, by this agent of Mercury, that messenger of the gods.

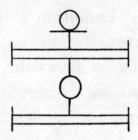

This is the sigil
of
Amethyst.

Avruthel, a treasure in thee do I find,
Thou healer of body and saviour of mind;
Thou medium of wisdom for me thou art given,
To carry the light and the healing from heaven.

THE CORAL

THE SUBJECT OF THIS ARTICLE WILL PROVE HIGHLY INTERESTING TO THE LOVER OF THE OCCULT, AND TO EVERY ADMIRER OF THE GOOD AND THE BEAUTIFUL IN NATURE.

I HAVE NO PUBLICATION IN MY POSSESSION WHICH TREATS OF THE CORAL SCIENTIFICALLY. HENCE, I MUST BE GUIDED, AND THAT ENTIRELY, BY MY OWN PSYCHIC INSTINCTS IN THESE MY OCCULT RESEARCHES, AS ON FORMER OCCASIONS WHEN SIMILARLY CIRCUMSTANCED. INDEED, AS A RULE, I AM EVER GUIDED BY MY OWN GENIUS, prompted by my own efforts of will; as, in all such occult matters I discard "guides" or teachers, for all that has ever been known of the Coral in the past, is faithfully preserved within those imperishable archives of nature, and that in such characters as I am able to decipher.

In the first place I would contradict an old notion entertained respecting the Coral, which is: that it is made up of the skeletons of defunct zoophites, the builders of the Coral; and, that the Coral is but the winding-sheet of these marvellous agents of the great Architect of the Universe. Such I consider as being a very low idea and a gross falsehood, and, consequently, misleading, as it is detracting from the wisdom and goodness of the Supreme Ruler; for, whatever may be the outwardly obvious in the eyes of the superficial observer, such is not the fact. The following is what I feel duly authorised to advance, and which I consider the incontrovertible truth. The Coral builders are androgenous — male and female, in one entity. Such are each and every agent of the Eternal ONE, which he may employ to build an animal, a plant, a tree, an island, or a world.

Be not alarmed at so strange an idea, for I am well aware that the popular notions are opposite to this, even science opposes this; but science depends on instruments in its observations, which, however perfect they might be supposed to be, they are not so perfect as to render the observer certain in such researches, that he is really on the line of truth.

The male and female idea as it is expressed at this day is, to all intents and purposes absurd, unphilosphical, and misleading. My statement stands thus: *The primal agent in the building of any kind of body, and of every species of organic life, is androgenous*. It is only as such that a creation can take place, and in no other way. The germ itself as it is given, is androgenous, and it is by virtue of this — *two in one* — that the germ builds for itself a body.

What is supposed to be the feminine in outer nature, is only so far a joint partner in the building, as to find, or to render, the necessary conditions. Thus in the present instance, and with reference to the Coral builder, it is androgenous. The water of the sea, or the ocean, is to it, what the feminine, outwardly considered, is to the animal or plant. It is, in short, the *nursing mother*. Those particles of which the Coral is composed, are held in solution in the water, and are thus taken up by this petrific giant of the deep. The law of elective affinity is as plainly made known in the feeding and building of the Coral, as in the feeding and building of all animal in its embryotic state, or a plant in its capsule, and subsequently in the earth. The Coral is as much the result of a growth, as the plant, the tree, or the animal.

I have only given hints on this subject, which are more suggestive than exhaustive. I am convinced that however much of novelty may be seen in these remarks, that what is here stated is philosophically correct. I advise the studious among my readers to take this subject up as a matter for serious thought during moments of calm reflection. For the present I am obliged to forgo the temptation to go further on these lines, as I must now treat of the virtues and influences of the Coral.

In modern times this gem has been considered far too common to deserve a place among precious stones. But the day is at hand when the long-neglected Coral will once more become a favourite. Had its virtues been known, the Coral would have been second to none at this day. The first of these virtues is: it is the antidote to that ossification which creeps on a person, and that prematurely. The person grows decrepid and prematurely old. The cartilagineous system that should have retained their elasticity and flexibility, becomes more or less ossified, and decrepitude follows, and takes the place of agility. The next property is: *a quickener of the senses*. That is, where there may be a partial or a more general numbness in the feeling, which is the obvious result of loss of power to retain vitality. I would here make a remark by way of correcting a notion, which is, that, when a person lacks vitality, they invariably attribute this to some other than the true cause. They accordingly make use of what they consider to be the best means for replenishing this loss, forgetting that the tissues need repairing, and that there is a consequent leakage. It is of no use putting water into a vessel full of holes, if you do so, the water will run out as fast, or nearly as fast, as it is put in; what is first of all necessary, is to stop up the holes and thus staunch the leakage. It is just so in such instances as are here alluded to: make the body life-proof, as you would make the vessel waterproof, and the cure is accomplished. What is here mentioned is as applicable to the thousands of the young, as to the aged.

Again, where there may be growing defect of eyes-sight, and that from a gradual loss of energy in the optic nerve, and not traceable to any acute form of disease, the Coral is the special remedy. The next property is, that the Coral is the strengthener of the mental faculties, and tends to preserve the mind from all those terrible and now hopeless complaints, which are on the increase among people of this, and of other so-called civilised countries.

Thus the Coral, if applied as I shall here point out, would prove one of the greatest blessings ever conferred on this country or age.

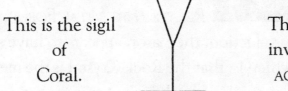

This is the sigil of Coral.

The word for invocation is
AG—ATH—EL.

AG—ATH—EL.

Agathel, most mighty, thou builder sublime!
Who raisest from atoms thy house in the deep;
A Building of God! it will triumph o'er time,
And amidst the rough billows securely can sleep.
Like thee would I build, like thee world I be.
Secure 'midst life's tempests—from weaknesses free.

THE ROCK CRYSTAL

I HAVE ELSEWHERE EXPRESSED MY VIEWS, OR WHAT I KNOW AS TO THE ORIGIN AND HISTORY OF THE CRYSTAL, AND THIS EXISTS IN THAT WORK OF MINE, *THE GEOZONIC SPHERES*.

BARON VON REICHENBACH, IN HIS GREAT WORK, ENTITLED, *RESEARCHES ON MAGNETISM, ELECTRICITY, HEAT, LIGHT, AND CHEMICAL ATTRACTION, IN THEIR RELATION TO VITAL FORCE*. IN THIS most elaborate production, the Baron appears to have solved a great problem, which is: that the Rock Crystal is the medium of a force which acts similarly to the magnet in its action on the nervous system; but that unlike the magnet, it has no attraction for iron or steel, or any of those substances which are affected by the magnet. Further, that the Crystal is not influenced in the least by the magnet, when rubbed by that instrument; or, when suspended freely, horizontally, is it affected by the magnetic meridian; hence, it follows, that whatever may be the influence which is produced by the Crystal, it is not magnetism any more

314

than that is magnetism which flows from the human hands or eyes, obedient to the human will. It is true we have got into the habit of calling nearly everything which lies outside, or beyond those limitations which mark off the domain of the ponderable — and which may be an active force, and capable of producing phenomena — Magnetism.

But this great Chemical Philosopher has proved, and that by repeated and incontestable proofs, that influences destitute of the properties of the magnet in all its phases, or familiar characteristics, are not to be classed as magnetic. At the same time such may partake of the character of a force, although having no sympathy with the magnet, and which is not magnetic. The Crystal is of this class, although it is incapable of attracting steel or iron, or even iron filings, or of being affected by the magnetic meridian.

Whatever may be capable of giving out an influence, must have the property of polarity; it must, in fact, have a north and a south pole. But, as the Crystal has no sympathy with the polarity of the earth, it would be improper to designate its poles as *north* and *south*. It must therefore be called *negative* and *positive* poles, for without polarity there can be no force, that is: no phenomenal force. This strange force which exists in the Crystal, Reichenbach called *Odyle* or *odylic* force, which in an early edition, a translation by Dr Ashburner, was called *Od* force, and I am inclined to look on the name *Odylic* as being applied subsequently, and as being considered by the translator more of a scientific term than the word *Od*. At the same time it is possible that the name *Odylic* is derived from *Od*. So far then does demonstrative science take us and no further. It will be my task in the present article, to make a move in advance of this.

To this end and by way of preparing the way for my higher purpose, I must state matters as clearly as possible. Whereas the magnet applies to the nerves of animals, as does the Crystal, it must possess that property or attribute which the Crystal possesses. But, it has a property which the Crystal has not; it can attract iron, or steel, and is capable of being affected by the magnetic meridian, or is in sympathy with the poles of the earth. The Crystal is not so, it is not susceptible to the magnetic meridian.

What I here state is the result of my study of this author, and, so far as the ideas involved in these my remarks may be concerned, they are found in this work. At the same time the wording is mine; hence, what I have written are not literal quotations, much less are they garbled quotations. But what do all these prove? They prove that the Rock Crystal is either in itself a source of influences, or, that it is a medium, or conductor of special influence, as pointedly, or as definitely as that of the human hand, or the human eye; for the crystal, philosophically considered, is, in reality, a living thing, a thing capable of holding a sympathetic intercourse with our present race; a thing which may, in the hands of a good and pure-minded person — one who has not been spoiled through the false teachings of this day — connect the soul of that person with the soul of the universe: and that apart from those peculiar powers of vision which the crystal is said to develop.

But to become all this, the mind should be as clear of all preconceptions as the crystal itself is clear of all but itself. There is what is designated the *Ovid* or egg-shaped crystal, which is said to be found native in some parts of India. But in the majority of such instances, these Ovids are manufactured out of glass. In the meantime they are said to answer as helps to mediumistic vision. With these I have nothing to do at present, as I am treating on the subject of the rock crystal as being recognised among the precious stones, and, if you can be *certain* that when you ask for the true Rock Crystal you get it, and not a bit of glass, you will find in it a valuable treasure. The crystal is not characterised by any one or more special properties, or, as being endowed with any one special attribute; but as a very wide or general application, more especially to the higher and more God-like powers of the soul. Nor can the crystal prove of any real benefit to that person whose mind may be engrossed with the ordinary matters of this everyday life, nor to those who are engaged in intellectual works, if such callings be but the mere mechanical studies of the hard and fast sciences; whose end and aim may be but some worldly purpose, and, which may be pressed into the services of that great god — Mammon. To such, the mere possession of the crystal as an ornament, cannot prove of any possible advantage. But to those who are guided by those spontaneous instincts of the soul, more than they are by their outer intellect, and are conscious of being the subjects of inspirations from sources unseen; indeed to all such as may be receptive, the crystal is of service.

The Rock Crystal is a safeguard against deception, or imposition from those whom you may have dealings with in life. This is most certainly a great boon, as it may liberate you from *too implicitly confiding* on the one hand, and an *unnecessary suspicion* on the other hand. If all were thus fortified, terrible crimes would be more rare. If your aspirations are heavenward, or God-ward, the crystal will prove of an inestimable value, but if you are intent on the accumulation of worldly wealth, and that *exclusively*, the crystal cannot benefit you.

This is the sigil
of
Rock Crystal.

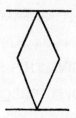

The word for invocation is
EV–AG–EL.

The pure in heart in Thee such will find
Light for the soul and peace for the mind;
Joy of heart, and freedom from care —
The truly confiding, need never despair.
Through Thee I may read the things of the past,
Thy records Divine for ever will last.
These records of Thine, O EV–AG–EL are true,
They are old as the ages, and yet they are new.
What has been, is now, and ever will be,
Thy light, O EV–AG–EL, give unto me.

THE EMERALD

THIS STONE, AS ITS NAME IMPLIES, IS OF A BEAUTIFUL GREEN, AND LIKE ITS NUMEROUS KINDRED OF GEMS, WAS A STONE FAMILIAR TO THE ANCIENTS. I SHALL, FURTHER ON IN THIS ARTICLE, GIVE THIS STONE IN THE LIGHT OF AN OLD PHILOSOPHY, THE RECORDS OF WHICH DO NOT EXIST ON THIS EARTH AT THE PRESENT DAY. BUT FOR THE PRESENT I WILL MENTION WHAT IS recorded of precious stones generally, and of the Emerald in particular, in the Bible. There are in this book several allusions to the Emerald, as well as to each of the other precious stones familiar to the people of modern times.

See Ezekiel 28:13 :

> "Thou hast been in Eden, the garden of God; every precious stone was thy covering, the Sardius, Topaz, and the Diamond, the Beryl, the Onyx, and the Jasper, the Sapphire, the Emerald, and the Carbuncle, and the Gold, &c."

Ezekiel 27:16 :

"Syria was thy merchant by reason of the multitude of the wares of thy making; they occupied in thy fairs with Emeralds, purple, and broidered work, and fine linen, and coral, and agate."

Revelation 4:3:

"And He that sat was to look upon like a jasper and a sardine stone; and there was a rainbow about the throne, in sight like unto an Emerald."

Revelation 21:19–20:

"And the foundations of the wall of the city were garnished with all manner of precious stones. The first foundation was Jasper, the second was Sapphire, the third a Chalcedony, the fourth an Emerald, the fifth a Sardonyx, the sixth Sardius, the seventh Chrysolyte, the eighth Beryl, the ninth a Topaz, the tenth a Chrysoprasus, the eleventh a Jacinth, the twelfth an Amethyst."

I now come to a description of the breastplate of the Jewish high-priest. This consisted of four rows of precious stones, and three in each row, which were as follows, each stone being a talisman for the name of each tribe (Exodus 28:17–18):–

| No. I. | A Sardius | — | a Topaz | — | and a Carbuncle. |
| Tribes: | Reuben | — | Simeon | — | and Levi. |

| No. II. | An Emerald | — | a Sapphire | — | and a Diamond. |
| Tribes: | Judah | — | Zebulum | — | and Issachar. |

No. III.	A Ligure	—	an Agate	—	and an Amethyst.
Tribes:	Dan	—	Gad	—	and Asher.

No. IV.	Beryl	—	an Onyx	—	and a Jasper.
Tribes:	Naphtali	—	Joseph	—	and Benjamin.

If you will turn to the 49th chapter of Genesis, there you will see an account of old Jacob telling the fortunes of his twelve sons, and by this fortune you may learn, to some extent, the influence of each of the twelve precious stones. But for the present it is the Emerald only that I am engaged with. And as this was Judah's stone, I shall in the first instance give you a quotation from the above-mentioned 49th chapter, of Judah's fortune as uttered by his old father, when near his death:

"Judah, thou art he whom thy brethren shall praise; thy hand shall be in the neck of thine enemies; thy father's children shall bow down before thee. Judah is a lion's whelp; from the prey, my son, thou art gone up; he stooped down, he couched as a lion, and as an old lion who shall rouse him up."

"The sceptre shall not depart from Judah, nor a law-giver from between his feet, until Shiloh come; and unto him shall the gathering of the people be."

"Binding his foal unto the vine, and his ass's colt unto the choice vine; he washed his garments in wine, and his clothes in the blood

322

of grapes; his eyes shall be red with wine, and his teeth white with milk."

It will be seen I have given Biblical quotations at some length, simply to show my resources, and that precious stones existed, and were recognised in the far past more than what they are at this day. But what very far transcends all this, the occult power which accompanies, or is otherwise embodied in precious stones, was known to the sages, priests, and prophets of the Bible. A portion of the old wisdom was then a living reality. That thing called civilization had not made its inroads into those sacred enclosures, and with bloody hands besmeared and defaced those records of wisdom which could be read in the sidereal heavens, and on rocks and rivers, and in purling brooks, in birds and beasts and creeping things, in forest trees and humble shrubs, in fruit trees bearing fruit; in the lightning and the thunder, whistling wind and the gale, the hurricane, and the wild tornado. From each and all these sages gathered wisdom, as the bees gather honey from each opening flower.

The next phase of this subject that will engage my attention, will be on psychic lines. I may go into some grand secrets respecting the Emerald, which may surpass all my present anticipations, I have already some such intimations.

The Emerald, as realised by me in its psychic and higher characteristics, has a history of far more sublime a character and of far more glorious a pedigree, than what is related of stone in mineralogical lore. Had this stone no special psychic history, it would never have had a terrestrial history, nor would it have had such prominence in sacred history.

The colour of the Emerald, and as connected with, or incorporated in this stone, is the virgin lute; that colour which first developed after the advent of light. This is the first-born out of the mystic purple, and which gave to this earth its first tinge, a tinge of living green! The voice which said "Let there be light," from heaven, was responded to from the earth: Let there be grass, or let there be verdure; for verdure cannot develop without light, it cannot develop in the dark. Life and a species of growth may take place in the dark, but not verdure. Man may live in the dark, but the bloom will depart from his cheeks, as bloom of health and verdure of earth go together, as both are governed by one and the same law. For where the one cannot exist, there the other disappears. This is therefore the most glorious, and the most Divine of every other colour. In the meantime, it does not follow, that because this stone possesses such properties, that it would be equally beneficial to us all, and that it would be an advantage to every one. It is a fact in nature—

and what may be founded on a law of nature is right — that if you would reap the advantages of certain influences, you have to adapt yourself to certain conditions, so as to become the recipient, beneficially, of such influences. This is more especially so with reference to the Emerald.

To one who may be living an animal life, more or less, or one whose sympathies are more with the artificial than the natural, or who may be a stranger to reflection, meditation, the spiritual or celestial magic, which is so prominently set forth and explained in this work. To all such this stone might be more inimical than otherwise; in such instances the tendencies would be to make the individual restless, ever on the move, ever seeking what he is not prepared to discover. But to one who may have strong aspirations for wisdom, that wisdom which is the wisdom of angels, and which guides into all truth; who seeks for their enlightenment from God and the soul-world, and who may be dissatisfied with the shams and hypocrisies of the present life, to such it would be a blessing. The blessing of old Jacob to his son Judah is yours.

By this blessing you will find that Judah represents all that is plentiful, a profusion of good things, kingly, and messianic. And if you refer to the breastplate of the high-priest, you will see that the Emerald was Judah's stone. You who possess this stone, or, in its absence, devote your mind to think of it, and conform to those conditions herein given, will receive its benefits, which are: divine wisdom, holy joy, benevolence of heart and a hungering and a thirsting for celestial communion, a renewal of your physical strength through the soul-world, and a possibility of attaining to a blessed immortality.

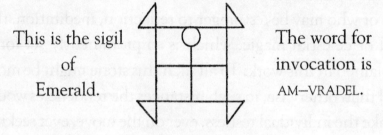

This is the sigil of Emerald.

The word for invocation is AM—VRADEL.

THE INVOCATION

Am-vradel! Thou Father, and Mother, one Divine;

Thou source of all power, which with beauty combine.

Earth's offspring of verdure, the first growth on this sod,

Thou jewel of Judah! and thou gem of the God.

Down deep in the earth, or the depths of the sea,

Wherever, Amvradel, thy body may be,

My soul in sympathy with thee will be join'd

By psychical searching, thy soul-self I shall find.

Hold up thou my life — thou of beauty the model —

Give me thy glory and thy wisdom, Amvradel.

THE DIAMOND

Its influence, and to whom it is applicable.

IT CAME FROM A REALM OF LIGHT,
WHERE DARKNESS HAD NEVER BEEN KNOWN;
FROM THENCE, IT FELL TO THIS EARTH,
BY THE BREATH OF STRANGE WINDS IT WAS BLOWN.

A LUMINOUS ETHER DIVINE,
ENFOLDED THIS EARTH WITH ITS SPAN;
MOST LUSTROUSLY THEN DID IT SHINE,
LONG AGES BEFORE THERE WAS MAN.

UNLIKE WAS THIS LIGHT TO THE SUN,
THE MOON COULD NOT MIMIC ITS RAYS;
BEFORE LIGHT DIURNAL BEGAN —
IT REIGN'D 'ERE THE FIRST BORN OF DAYS.

The above poem is given me, inspirationally, and I consider it in the light of an authentic utterance respecting the origin and properties of the Diamond.

This poem I take for my text, on which I found a few remarks — such remarks as will prove suggestive at least, although they may not be considered scientifical.

In the first place the source of the Diamond is light.

"It came from a realm of light."

This light was a light in itself, and not a mere reflection of a light. It originated *in itself*. What we call darkness is not darkness in relation to this light, and on the other hand, what we call darkness is light to this, or in its relationship with this, and what we call light is darkness to this comparison. This light never fluctuates. It never ebbs and flows by way of intermittency or change. It is, in fact, elementary light. It was in the domain of this Divine luminosity that the Diamond became compressed into the hardest of substances It has no sympathy with artificial lights of any kind. Nor is this gem combustible under any ordinary degree of heat. It is *not* pure carbon, as stated by chemists. It is as far from being carbon, "as thrice from the centre to the utmost pole;" and, although the hardest of substances, it is not a metal, nor can it be defined as a stone.

In the meantime, it is a gem or jewel of the highest significance and of tremendous importance. It came to this earth from the upper and outer mundane spheres, governed by the laws of gravity. At the same time, there were *"Strange Winds,"* or influences from intelligences, by whose agencies these starlike gems were scattered abroad. They fell to the earth, but not as meteors fall, for the Diamond is not a meteoric stone, as it comes not from a meteoric source.

> "A *luminous ether Divine,*
> *Enfolded this earth with its span.*"

And God said: "Let there be light." This light was not *made* or *created*. The passage does not convey to the mind of the intelligent reader such an idea; for it is, in fact, uncreated, it is coeval with the Absolute. The Divine Will simply commanded the light, this primal light, to shine out of darkness. This was that mystic dove which brooded over the face of the deep, "and made it pregnant." It manifested itself by an eternal and unchangeable law or decree.

This light is that which is concealed at the centre of every world and sun in the universe, and which I discovered at the centre of this earth, and which presented itself to me as the "Primal Globe." This light is in sympathy with the sun; that is, with the true primal light of the sun. Both combined do constitute the true life of the world; not the life which depends on combustion, or which is developed through combustion. This is known by the phrase, "Animal life," which is apparently founded on laws which appear to me the perversion of the law of the true life. The condition which renders this perverted life possible, has been developed through the action of some third or intermediary power, connected with surface-cruet conditions of this globe. This surface-crust has been during nearly the past 6,000 years, the play-ground of forces. The end, or seeming aim, of such forces is *death*, or destruction, or nullification of the grand but now hidden law of the true life.

The Diamond is a gem, by virtue of its homogeneity, and belongs to the domain of the true life! This is a revelation that has *never* before been made known to this race! Hence it follows that the Diamond is *sacred*, one of the *most* sacred: yes, *the* most sacred of all gems. It is sad to think of it being handled so irreverently, and even *profanely*, by mere vulgar men of the world, whose portion is in this life. The Diamond has a power, when in the possession of Kings, Monarchs, Presidents of Republics, Princes, Lords, Nobles, Legislators, Judges in the Courts of Law, Magistrates, and all State Authorities; also very advanced Occultists, or those who are entitled to the degree of adept-ship. But no army officer, or naval officer, or professional slayer of men or animals, nor should any instrument such as swords, daggers, or any instruments which but *represent* those intended to kill, be ever decorated with the Diamond.

I am not allowed to give Word and Sigil for this gem.

THE RUBY

I intend giving some practical information respecting the Ruby, which will embrace some of the characteristical properties, or distinguishing marks observable in the true stone, and the absence of these in the manufactured ones. Also, as to the possibility for an ordinary person without scientific attainments being placed in a position for distinguishing between the genuine stone, and the counterfeit, and thus tend to some extent, at least, to render fraudulency more difficult and less remunerative. What I here give may be tested, and should the following tests prove satisfactory, then I hope that credit will be awarded to whom it is due. It is not a pleasing thought to harbour, that one is imposed on, even in the matter of a jewel. The false jewel may appear as beautiful as the genuine, but after all, if you pay for the stone, you should not be supplied with the paste one.

The Test

The genuine stone is not free from small clouds or hazes at some point or other, as a consequence of its laminaferious nature;

for all stones entitled to the name of precious stones, are more or less laminar, and such may appear at different angles. This being the case it necessarily follows that transparency complete, or perfect, is impossible, owing to the interception of the different angles, whence arises the cloud or haze. All these may pass unnoticed by the casual observer. To render the process of inspection practicable to all, I offer the following suggestions:

Get a round goblet glass free from cuts or marks of any kind. Place your stone within the bottom of the glass, at the centre. Then fill the glass with clear water; allow the daylight to fall on the glass, and keep it clear of the shades of outside things. Also, keep clear of direct sunshine. Your stone will now be magnified so as to enable you to see such marks in it as you could not see otherwise, as the magnifying power will be equal at all points. If you find your stone laminated, and a haze at some point, you may infer it to be the true Ruby. The paste one cannot be made to contain these characteristics; consequently the paste will appear more brilliant than the true stone, but, more glassy.

The Psychological Properties of the Ruby

It is more than probable there may be a few of my readers who will not find it convenient to become the actual possessor of the Ruby, seeing it is among the most precious of gems. There are those who possess this jewel, with several others, but who may not know the real occult value which lies in what they possess. I give to each and all who read my volume, an information by which he may avail himself of the occult virtues of the Ruby, whether he be a possessor or not of the materialized one. These properties are made known to me by revelations.

The Virtues of the Ruby

Are you the subject of some grievous trial? Is your grief of a heart-rending character? Are your pangs those of bereavement, or that of some terrible disappointment? Do you realise your condition as being hopeless? Direct your mind to the Ruby. Think of the living Ruby. Direct your thoughts to this gem. And the love, the peace, the comfort of your God will meet you there. Those hidden virtues of the Ruby will attract to itself the burden of your sorrows, and the cause of your sighs and tears. Your God through this, his beautiful little agent will soothe your agitations, he will disburden your oppressed soul. Look to this Sigil, and repeat the following word nine times, DER–GAB–EL.

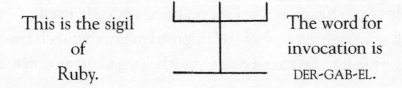

This is the sigil of Ruby.   The word for invocation is DER-GAB-EL.

THE TURQUOISE

THIS STONE IS DESIGNATED A PERSIAN GEM, BUT WAS FIRST IMPORTED TO EUROPE FROM TURKEY. AS A GEM, IT MAY NOT HOLD A FIRST PLACE, IN POINT OF VALUE: THAT IS, AS AN ARTICLE OF COMMERCE; BUT IF VALUED FROM A PSYCHIC POINT OF VIEW, IT STANDS ALONE AS BEING PRE-EMINENTLY THE STONE OF ALL OTHERS — UNIQUE. THE CHEMIST MAY TREAT THE MATTER LIGHTLY, IN SAYING THAT ITS COMPONENT PARTS ARE BUT COMMON, AND WELL-KNOWN substances: the phosphate of alumina, oxide of iron, and copper. Just so, scientists tell us what are the primary elements of living tissue, both in plant and animal, each and nearly all are common, that is they are quite familiar to us. But the question arises— what is that which permeates those tissues? There is evidently an influence proceeding from that being who is made up of these common materials; this influence produces sensations, or is capable of producing sensations on beings outside itself.

But some one may say, or feel disposed to say, that such tissues are *living* tissues, and that living tissues belong to organic matter, that the properties of the vegetable and animal kingdoms are the properties which belong to organic matter; that life itself is essentially the prime characteristic of organic matter; but that a stone is not organic matter. This scrupulous suggestion at first sight may appear plausible; but to what lengths may the investigator proceed on the lines of the most careful enquiry, in order he may discover that line of demarcation where the organic ends, and the inorganic begins? Can any scientist say he has plumbed the depths of the lowest forms of organic matter, so as to say there is no organic matter beyond this point? I think not. The stone at some epoch in the far past, glomorated, and became an homogeneous substance, which took place on those lines which determine the outward forms of vegetable and animal life.

To have done so, there must have been an inner principle, an agent, which acted attractively, and selectively, to bring into one mass the requisite material for the building up of a class of stone, having such and such a characteristic as may suffice to identify that stone as one of a peculiar type, and which, after all, may prove but a species of a class.

It is thus that not only has a stone a life principle, but that it possesses something higher and of a very subtle nature. The tree has not only a life principle, but it possesses higher properties, as I have already pointed out in former articles. The Turquoise is a living, organised bit of matter, whose properties or attributes are as follows: It is a very sympathetic stone, its sympathies are allied with the mystical in every department of nature, but more especially with those mysteries which are concealed in the crust of the earth, and also in the mineral kingdom, also to those mystic properties concealed in metallic substances. In the meantime it possesses other and yet higher properties than these. It tends to connect the soul of the one who can meditate and contemplate with the universal soul, and that *consciously*, so that the individual consciousness becomes more or less identified with the universal. The Turquoise tends towards the development of those inner powers which I have been developing during these five-and-forty years. But to him whose life is in the ordinary swim of the great crowd, and who is a stranger to secret prayer and secret contemplation, accompanied with profound meditation and calm reflection, to such an one neither the Turquoise nor any other mystical instrument can be of any value. But to the thoughtful and meditative person it will prove an invaluable treasure.

This is the sigil
of
Turquoise.

The word for
invocation is
HAR-VAL-AM.

THE SAPPHIRE

REGARDING THE NATURAL PROPERTIES OF THE SAPPHIRE, I HAVE BUT LITTLE TO SAY BEYOND THIS: IT IS A GEM OF A CLEAR BRIGHT BLUE, OR SKY BLUE, AND IS NEXT THE DIAMOND IN VALUE. IT IS A GEM THAT WAS RECOGNISED BY THE WISE MEN OF THE PAST. THE SAGES OF ANCIENT ASSYRIA WERE FAMILIAR WITH THE SAPPHIRE, AND THAT PRIOR TO THE EGYPTIAN CIVILISATION. ALSO by the sages of China, Assyria, and Egypt, the Sapphire was held to be the representative of a power in nature, peculiarly its own. Not only so, but that the gem being pellucid and partly self-luminous, was generated by powers which operate in the darkest recesses of nature, and as such, is as much an organic entity as the plant or tree. The scientists of our day know

337

absolutely *nothing* respecting the origin of this and other gems. What they offer is suppositional or conjectural. What I am authorised to offer is: that the gems abound on, and in this earth today, are relics of a past mundane state, when this earth was a far more glorious world than it is at this day. The new heaven and the new earth alluded to in the 21st chapter of the Revelations of John, is simply what the seer realised, by virtue of his having ascended to that stratum of thought pictures which hang on and ornament the walls of those imperishable spheres which exist in their idealistic state, as mementoes of what were once developed glories on the outer plane, of an earth-life as it was then realised. The city which the seer saw coming down from God out of heaven, he designates the "New Jerusalem," hence was not the Jerusalem of that day in which the seer lived, for it is called the *New* Jerusalem. Its dimensions do exceed that of any other city, or, indeed that of any other country or continent, and that without encroaching on a sea or an ocean, so that the surface of the globe must pass through another geological change ere it can be prepared for such a development, or become the theatre of such a realisation.

The prophet saw it coming down from God out of the heaven. The word heaven, in this and several other parts of this book, denotes the mystical spaces in nature. Thus when we read the phrase: "And heaven opened, &c.," it imports some new development on the earth. And what is this new development, but a repetition of what has been, so that whatever this earth may have been countless millions of years ago, the same will again be realised in the interminable future, as all movements are within a circle, and not a straight line. At the same time each of those grand revolutions will not repeat itself *in that very same groove*, any more than the planets do repeat themselves by moving in the *exact groove*, in each of their revolutions, each one is a *fraction* nearer the sun. This pervades the whole of time, and space, through what we call *eternity*. Thus it comes to pass that the gems and jewels of the past, which are now concealed within the earth, by a power which preserves them until that day when the New Jerusalem comes down from God (or the Gods), out of heaven. That day when the "Tabernacle of God will be among the men of that glorious reign, and when tears shall cease to flow and there shall be no more death, and sorrow and crying shall be no more." Then from the 18th verse of that said chapter to the 21st verse, you have all the precious stones set forth in their order. Then shall the precious stones once more become the variegated glories of a jewelled world. This earth will once more have attained its majority. Then shall each stone in its turn, occupy its legitimate place, and discharge its peculiar mission. There are parts of this earth where the precious stones abound, beyond all our present conceptions of profusion. But they are hidden in that place where wisdom might be found, and that same question which was asked by that sage: "Where shall wisdom be found," might with equal propriety be put forth, and where may these gems of the gods be found, the place is not known today, at least, not to the men of this world, who have their portion in this life.

The Virtues of the Sapphire

It is a cure for doubt and despondency. It is a reviver of hopes that have been blighted. It deprives the future of its dread, and renders the dark valley of death, redolent with sunshine. In a well developed mind it sheds a hallow, and begets sensations unlike anything we may have realised. If the mind be sufficiently tranquil and free from any special bias, just contemplate the Sigil, and repeat the name and invocation for a few times, and you will partake of a joy which will surpass every other joy of your life.

This is the sigil
of
Sapphire.

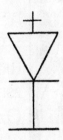

The word for invocation is

TROO-AV-AL.

THE INVOCATION.

A voice from the Sapphire came unto me —
Come hither my child, come hither and see.
With me it is day, I know of no night,
My sky's ever clear, my sun's ever bright.
No weeping, no mourning, no shedding of tears,
No change in my seasons, no counting of years.
One thousand years with me is one day;
My work is *all* pleasure, my labour is play.
Would'st thou be happy? would'st thou be free?

THE RED GARNET

THIS STONE CONTAINS VIRTUES SPECIALLY PECULIAR TO ITSELF, OR WHAT MAY NOT BE DISCOVERABLE IN ANY OTHER STONE, PLANT, OR TREE. I AM HERE ALLUDING MORE ESPECIALLY TO THAT SPECIES OF GARNET CALLED THE RED GARNET. IT IS FOUND MOST COMMONLY IN MICA, *SLATE*, *HORNBLEND*, *SLATE*, AND *GNEISS*. THE NAME SEEMS TO have been derived from the Latin, "granum" — seed. This idea may have come from the supposed fact that this stone is a combination of crystalline grains, adhering together from affinity. This would lead one to suppose the pre-existence of a principle, a living principle, a divine principle, a soul, in fact, which collected those grains together in the same way, or by the same law, as the plant or the tree, or as animal life builds up an animal structure, designated an organism.

We are accustomed to call all mineral substances *inorganic matter*; in the meantime, such is not so in those primal formations which we discover among the mineral and metallic substances abounding in and on this earth. But when these substances are transformed by the hand of man, and their primitive structure broken up, the vital principle is no longer there, any more than the life principle remains in a tree when it has been cut up and transformed into chairs and tables.

The primal basis on which I build this new philosophy, if it may be called such, is: that every mineral substance, as well as every vegetable substance, has a living principle, soul, or genius; and it is by virtue of this soul or genius that the stone is marked by certain characteristics, and contains certain properties, such as may be capable of acting on other substances or other organisms, and of producing changes in each.

This is my first thesis. My next is: that in order to become the subject of the stone's influence, it is necessary we should become sympathetically connected with that stone, plant, or tree; not by first *killing* it and subsequently by taking portions in pills, powders, or decoctions; but by realising a sympathetic union with the stone, plant, or tree; and that by a kind of fascination, which you may designate love, towards that object. It is a law in nature, that whatever you *greatly* admire, and that, freely, or spontaneously, you love after a fashion; and what you love, or greatly admire, you become negative towards that object, and becoming thus negative, you must of necessity become receptive of whatsoever influences that thing may be capable of imparting.

It is well-known that you cannot force yourself to admire anything, but must be first of all fascinated by, or through, an inspiration. This inspiration is the precursor of fascination, and follows as the result of calm or quiet contemplation.

I have already presented my readers with a vast number of resources, by which you may meet, and overcome, the various ills that flesh and blood are heir to. These are no idle fancies on my part, but are veritable truths. These are revelations which have been lying within the archives of the universe for thousands of years before our history awoke to meet the concurrent events of a time comparatively modern. We have straggling hints, or references, to peoples or nations who are said to have worshipped trees. Indeed some traces of such a kind of idolatry appears to be easily found among what are called the rude and barbaric tribes. These are but the remains of what was once a glorious philosophy.

I, Charubel, am the ordained instrument to publish to this race, now to the sear of its life, this divine philosophy. However you may feel disposed to treat this subject, depend on it, there is no other messenger born, or yet within the folds of a distant future, who will publish again this philosophy further than he may seek to call the attention of the world to what I have written.

I do not say these things in the spirit of a proud boaster, but simply in the spirit of truth and righteousness.

Now what I have written in this article might appear a digression from the subject in hand, viz.: the Garnet, but it is not so. What I have written is the result of my psychic contemplation of this wonderful gem. The influence of this stone on my mind is that of inspiration. It may not have exactly the same effect on every one that it has on me, at the same time you will feel a power or an influence whilst contemplating the Garnet, especially when the mind is aided by the ritual which I hope being able to give you; for with the aid of this ritual you may be able to dispense with the stone itself. This stone, among other uses, is a special remedy for, and a protection from, all diabolical influences. There is no infernal power that can injure the person who uses this ritual, faithfully and in consciousness of the direct presence of the Lord God of host.

This is the sigil
of
the Red Garnet.

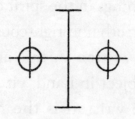

The word for invocation is

AR–HU–GAL.

THE INVOCATION

O Thou, great Builder, of the stupendous whole:

Within each creature bast Thou bestow'd a soul.

By virtue of this wisdom, and power of Thy own,

Hast Thou bestow'd a genius in the Garnet stone;

Through which a light I may receive from Thee.

The blessing of being from powers infernal free.

AR–HU–GAL! thee for ever, and for ever, I adore,

To Thee I give hosannas evermore.

THE CARBUNCLE

THIS STONE BELONGS TO THE GARNET FAMILY, AT THE SAME TIME IT IS OF A MUCH DEEPER RED THAN THE GARNET.

I AM NOT INFORMED BY WRITERS ON THE SUBJECT AS TO THE CHARACTERISTIC SHAPE OF THIS STONE WHEN FOUND IN ITS NATIVE STATE OR PRIMITIVE CONDITION. I HAVE SEEN A FEW SPECIMENS OF THIS STONE, ONE IN A RING AND THE OTHER IN A PEAR-SHAPE FORM, resembling in colour and shape big drops of blood. This shape impressed me very forcibly with the notion that possibly this may have been one of its primitive forms; at the same time I do not suppose that the Carbuncle, any more than the Garnet, is confined to any one form, and that exclusively. Nor is this of any special importance to me in giving to this age the secret virtues of this stone. It is with the psychic influence of the Carbuncle that I am concerned.

The soul of the Carbuncle, as revealed to me by certain symbols. The symbol gives me inspirations to the effect that this stone is related more especially to the things of time and sense, and such matters as may concern us most in our everyday intercourse with mankind and with the world in general.

347

Physically it strengthens and vivifies the vital and the generative forces in human nature. Its influences partake to a considerable degree of that of the trine aspect of Mars with the moon, modified by a ray from Jupiter.

Hence I conclude that the Carbuncle will benefit those who may be lacking in energy, and who may be suffering from *anaemia*. Also those who may be in want of that animal courage, a courage which is so necessary in our dealings with a hard and unsympathetic world. It tends to render us regardless of sympathy. It also tends to sharpen our business propensities, and thus make us more successful in all business transactions. To the dull, the lethargic, and the sluggish lymphatic, and people of cold habits, this stone would prove an invaluable treasure.

This is the sigil of Carbuncle.

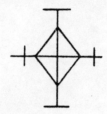

The word for invocation is APH-RU-EL.

THE INVOCATION

Hither lead me, thither guide me,
In this mortal life below;
In my weakness stand beside me,
Save me from my daily foe.
APH-RU-EL, all omnipotent to me,
In this name I all shall conquer;
At this sigil my foes shall flee.
In my sickness and my sorrow,
Thou doest give thy balsam free;
Heal the of my present weakness,
That I better days shall see.

INDEX

INDEX OF TREES, SHRUBS,

PLANTS, MINERALS AND

PRECIOUS STONES.

Adder's Tongue *Ophioglossum* : Dispeller of General Torpor and Gloom, and Listless Apathy.

Ash Tree *Fraxinus* : Acute pain in the Chest. Affections of the Bronchia. Remedy for Tumours, Abscesses, and Chronic Excrescences of the Skin.

Anemone (Wild) *Ranunculo* : (Negative) Valvular Affections of the Heart. Gouty Pains in various parts of the Body. Hemicrania, accompanied with great Heat in Left Cheek and Temples, and Hot Tears from the Eyes. Inflamed Kidneys.

Alder Tree *Ae'nus Glutinoso* : To break up old associations and old friends and relationships is an isolating character. (Use with caution). Disconnect the mind from the past, and long-standing Ulcers and Tumours, etc. Good for the Hermit or Recluse.

Brook-Lime *Veronica-Beccalunga* : Spinal Irritation. Restlessness. Sleeplessness, accompanied with a Dead Ache in the Head. Spinal Chord and Lower Brain, also the Nerves of Nutrition generally.

Buttercup *Ranunculus* : Melancholy and a Looking-back, and Longing for Past Scenes and Old Home, People who Weep from Gloom. Departed Friends. Unrealised Anticipations and Suicidal Tendencies. Great Heat in the Face and Forehead. Inflamed Eyes, etc.

Birch Tree *Betula'ceœ* : Restlessness and Nervous Irritability, accompanied with great anxiety. See the entry for Birch Tree and use of a Decoction for a Stimulant of the Brain.

Box Tree *Bux'us Sempervi'rens* : Acute Constrictive Pain about Breast Bone, attended with anxiety, difficulty of Breathing, and sense of Suffocation. A Strengthener and Fortifier of Chest and Lungs.

Celandine *Chilido'nium Majus* : *See Poppy Family*

Clematis *Crowfoot Family* : (Negative) An Inflamed Groin. Intense Pains in Legs and Thighs. Acrid Virus in the Blood. Germinal Scrofula.

Christmas Rose *Crowfoot Tribe* : In all cases of Insanity or any tendency that way through Excitement, Worry, or Anxiety.

Crimson Corn Poppy *Papaver Rhœas* : Deep Dull Pain in Forehead (Centre) with great heaviness about Eyes and Eyelids. A great want of Sleep, and unrest after Sleep.

Averse to labour or work, living in a kind of Stupor State, not unlike the effect of a Narcotic.

Crane's Bill or Herb Robert *Geranium Family* : Astringent for Laxity of the Nervous System. Loss of Tone and Vitality. Toothache, etc.

Devil's Bit *Scabiosa Succisa* : A Soul Blight, the result of Psychic Parasites.

Elder Tree *Sambucus-nigra* : (Negative). For persons of Gross Habits, and where there are tendencies towards Vices of Low and Animal Character. Lust and Animality.

Elm Tree *Ulmus Campestris* : (Negative). Strengthener of Brain and Nerves and other symptoms. Extreme Languor, and Sense of Prostration and Softening of Brain.

Ferns *Filices* : Heart Strengthener, acting powerfully on the Arterial System, and Chest Affections arising from Weakness.

Fern (Wall) *Polypodium* : Weak action of the Heart. Atrophy (general weakness with wasting).

Fir Tree *Coniferea* : (Positive). General Languor. Oppressive Feeling of Exhaustion. A Sallow Complexion, arising from a sluggish liver. A weak and intermittent pulse and feeling of fullness.

Holly Tree *I'lex Aquifolium* : Great Heat in the Throat. Constrictive and Cramp-like Feeling about the region of the Heart. Spinal Affections. Virulent Pains in the Head with great Heat. Intermittent Fever. Delirium Tremens, etc.

Heather (Common) *Calluna Vulgaris* : (Medicinal Virtues): — Inordinate Discharges from the Bladder or Intestines and such as experience Numbness of Limbs, and more especially extremities. Note—Tincture for Paralysed Limbs. Slow Action of Heart.

(Psychic Virtues):—Intrepidity in presence of danger. Fearlessness of Death. Settled state of mind to one purpose. Great Robustness of Health of Body.

Ivy *He'dera He'lix* : Over-excited Brain. Hallucination. Sleeplessness from over-excitement, etc.

Lichen *Cryptogamia Class* : Leprosy. Scaly Skin Diseases, Poison in the Blood after Scarlatina.

Lilac *Olive Tribe* : Heart Affections, where too Quick and Feeble.

Lime Tree *Tilia Europoa* : Weakness, a Gradual Sinking, when food taken yields no support. Lime tree specific remedy for depletion and want of vigour after long illness, providing the food which the sinking soul requires. A giver of Strength and Vigour.

Mosses : An Antidote for Vagaries. False Delusive Visions. Despondency. Hallucinations and Melancholy of every cast. Suicidal Tendencies

Mares-Tail *Hippuris* : Bodily Infirmity through Obesity, etc.

Monk's Hood *Crowfoot Tribe* : Colds and Chills after Perspiration.

Mallow Family *Althœ'a Officinalis* : Hay Fever, extraordinary discharge from nose with frequent sneezings, attended with restlessness, a cure for Influenza.

Mountain Ash *Pyrus Aucupa'ria* : (Negative). The Gout. Uric Acid. Rheumatism. An attractor of the Poison which causes Gout and Rheumatism.

Oak Tree *Quercus Robur* : Prostration after Illness an all-gone Feeling. A giving up and great Timidity, and Dread of Death. The strengthening influence of this Tree for the prostrate invalid is very great.

Orange Tribe *Aurantiaceœ* : Discords on Soul Plane. Friction, etc. Sorrow and Grief. Melancholy.

Pæony *Crowfoot Tribe* : Generation of Life Forces through the Spleen, for people Suffering from Great Weakness, accompanied with a sense of Prostration on least exertion. Kind of Sinking without Pain.

Poppy Family — Celandine : Eruption and Skin Diseases of all kinds.

Poplar Tree *Populus Nigra* : Want of Will Power. Loss of Memory. Dullness of Apprehension. Weak or Imperfect Eyesight. Deafness arising from Constitutional Weakness, and all symptoms which pertain to the Digestive, Assimilative Secretion, Absorption, etc., and all those offices requiring the healthy action of the Stomach, Liver, Kidneys, and Bowels.

St John's Wort *Hypericaceæ* : A Strengthener, Healer, and Comforter of the Soul. A sensation of Floating, no Rest day or night— Insomnia — Excessive Irritability, a temper ever out of joint. A fear of some unknown trouble about to overtake you, and Suicidal Tendencies.

Wood-Sorrel (Common) *Oxalis-acetosella* : (Positive). Cancers. Tumours. A Life-giver, a Vitalizer, and Internal Invigorator, for people who have been long ill, etc.

Yew Tree : A Soul Strengthener, and Healer of the Poor and Dejected. Lowness of Spirits and Great Depression, a Weak Soul. Remains of that Morbid Effluvia, which, like a horrid nightmare, clings to the helpless soul.

INDEX OF MINERALS

Copper : A Soul Strengthener, etc.

Gold : Giver of Health and Long Life. Oppression and Spirit Drooping. Troubled and Worried. Disheartened and Helpless and Despair. Good for Sluggish Natures where action of Heart too Slow. Persons who are averse to an active life. The Lymphatic Temperament. The Anæmics The Indolent and Putter-off till tomorrow. The Aged.

Iron (Elemental) : (Positive). Persons of Pale Sallow Complexion, of a Cold Nature, with Poor Blood. The Full Blooded and Poor Blooded people should not use only under very careful circumstances and conditions.

INDEX OF PRECIOUS STONES

Amethyst : False Vision and Degenerating Memory. Colour Blindness, etc.

Coral : Decrepit persons and prematurely old. A Quickener of the Senses. Good in growing defect of Eyesight from gradual loss of energy in the Optic Nerve (which is not traceable to any acute form of disease) is a special remedy. A Strengthener of the Mental Faculties.

Carbuncle : Physically Strengthens and Vivifies the Vital and Generative Forces in human nature, for the lacking of Energy and the Sufferers from Anæmia, and those who are in want of animal courage. Tendency to render us regardless of sympathy. Sharpener of Business Propensities. Invaluable treasure to the Dull, Lethargic, and the Sluggish Lymphatic, and people of Cold Habits.

Diamond : For Kings, Monarchs, Presidents, and people of high standing, etc. State Authorities, and the advanced Occultists.

Emerald : For those who aspire to Wisdom and seek Enlightenment, and those who seek the good of life, etc.

Rock Crystal : Safeguard against Deception or Imposition, and for those who think of a better life and the pure in heart.

Ruby : (Negative). Most Precious of Gems. Grevious Trial. Hopeless condition, etc. Heart-rending Grief. Pangs of Bereavement. Terrible Disappointment. Soother of Agitation and Disburdener of the Oppressed Soul.

Red Garnet : Inspiration. Remedy for Diabolical Influences, etc.

Sapphire : Cure for Doubt and Despondency. Reviver of Hopes that have been blighted. Disperses the future of its dread, and renders the Valley of Death redolent with sunshine.

Topaz : Applies to Fair People with Weak or Fragile Constitutions, and inclined to become Despondent and of Cold Habits. A help to those who are out of sight and behind the scenes, or in the shade. It begets hopefulness in the hopeless. Strengthens and Fortifies the Soul against the evil and wicked persons.

Turquoise : Sympathetic Stone. A connector of Souls. Developer of Inner Powers. Invaluable treasure to the thoughtful and meditative.

INDEX OF DISEASES AND AILMENTS

CURABLE BY THE PSYCHIC VIRTUES OF

TREES, SHRUBS, PLANTS, MINERALS

AND PRECIOUS STONES

To be read in conjunction with the Index of trees, shrubs, plants, minerals and precious stones. Once the disease or ailment has been located read the corresponding index entry for the tree, shrub, plant, etc., together with the relevant section in the main text in order to full comprehend the overall attributes.

ENVIRONMENT

Poor and Dejected, Healer of the	Yew Tree
Suicidal Tendencies	Mosses
Vices of Low and Animal Character	Elder Tree
Work or Labour, Aversion to	Poppy, Crimson Corn

MENTAL

Anticipations, Unrealised	Buttercup
Anxiety	Birch Tree, Box Tree
Anxiety, A tendency to Insanity from	Christmas Rose
Apathy	Adder's Tongue
Bad-tempered	St John's Wort
Brain, Over-excited	Ivy
Cold Nature, Persons of	Iron (Elemental)
Death, Dread of	Oak Tree
Death, Fearlessness of	Heather, (Psychic Virtues)
Depression, Lowness of Spirits and	Yew Tree
Depression: Oppression and Spirit Drooping	Gold
Despair	Gold
Despondency	Mosses, Sapphire
Disappointment	Ruby
Doubt, Cure for	Sapphire
Dullness of Apprehension.	Poplar Tree
Enlightenment	Emerald

Excitement, A tendency to Insanity from	Christmas Rose
Fear	St John's Wort
Fearlessness of Death	Heather, (Psychic Virtues)
Floating, A sensation of	St John's Wort
Frail — Fair Persons inclined to become Despondent and of Cold Habits	Topaz
General Health, Great Robustness of Health of Body	Heather, (Psychic Virtues)
Gloom	Adder's Tongue
Gloom, People who Weep from	Buttercup
Hallucination	Ivy, Mosses
Hermit	Alder Tree, Sapphire
Hope, Reviver of	Topaz
Indolency	Gold
Infirm — Fair Persons inclined to become Despondent and of Cold Habits	Topaz
Insanity	Christmas Rose
Intrepidity in presence of danger	Heather, (Psychic Virtues)
Irritability	St John's Wort
Langour, General	Fir Tree, Elm Tree
Lethargy	Pæony
Listlessness	Adder's Tongue
Melancholy	Buttercup, Mosses, Orange Tribe
Memory, Loss of	Poplar Tree

Mind, Settled state of	Heather, (Psychic Virtues)
Morbidity	Yew Tree
Nervous Irritability	Birch Tree
Prostration on least exertion	Pæony
Recluse	Alder Tree
Restlessness	Birch Tree
Sleeplessness from over-excitement	Ivy
Sorrow	Orange Tribe
Spleen, Generation of Life Forces through the	Pæony
Suicidal Tendencies	Mosses, St John's Wort, Buttercup
Torpor	Adder's Tongue
Trepidation	St John's Wort
Troubled and Worried	Gold
Vagaries, An Antidote for	Mosses
Visions, False Delusive	Mosses, Amethyst
Weak or Fragile Fair Persons inclined to become	
Despondent and of Cold Habits	Topaz
Weakness: A sinking without pain.	Pæony
Will Power, Lack of	Poplar Tree
Will, Lack of — A giving up and great Timidity	Oak Tree
Wisdom	Emerald
Work or Labour, Aversion to	Poppy, Crimson Corn
Worry	Gold
Worry, A tendency to Insanity from	Christmas Rose

PHYSICAL

Abscess	Ash Tree
Aged, Help for	Gold
Ageing Prematurely	Coral
Anaemia	Gold
Anaemia: Physically Strengthens and Vivifies the Vital and Generative Forces	Carbuncle
Appetite: a Gradual Sinking, when food taken yields no support.	Lime Tree
Arterial System	Ferns
Atrophy — Weakness with Wasting	Wall Fern
Bladder, Inordinate Discharges from	Heather (Medicinal Virtues)
Blood Poisoning after Scarlatina	Lichen
Blood, Acrid Virus in the	Clematis
Blood, Poor	Amethyst
Bowels	Poplar Tree
Brain — Stimulant (used as a decoction)	Birch Tree
Brain (lower)	Brook-Lime
Brain, Softening of	Elm Tree
Brain, Strengthener of	Elm Tree
Breathing, Difficulty of	Box Tree
Bronchia	Ash Tree
Cancers	Wood-Sorrel
Cheek(left) and Temples, Great heat in the	Anemone

Eyesight: growing defect from gradual loss of energy in the Optic Nerve	Coral
Eyes, Hot tears from the	Anemone
Eyes, Inflamed	Buttercup
Face and Forehead, Great Heat in the	Buttercup
Fever, Intermittent	Holly Tree
Forehead (Centre), Deep Dull Pain in	Poppy, Crimson Corn
Frail — Decrepit Persons	Coral
Fullness, Feeling of	Fir Tree
Germinal Scrofula	Clematis
Gout	Mountain Ash
Gout Pains	Anemone
Groin, Inflamed	Clematis
Hallucination	Ivy
Hay Fever	Monk's Hood
Headache	Brook-Lime
Head, Virulent Pains in the	Holly Tree
Hearing, Loss of	Poplar Tree
Heart Affections, where too Quick and Feeble	Lilac
Heart Strengthener	Ferns
Heart, Weakness of the	Wall Fern
Heart Valves	Anemone
Heartbeat	Fir Tree

Nerves of Nutrition	Brook-Lime
Nerves, Strengthener of	Elm Tree
Nervous System, Astringent for Laxity of the	Crane's Bill
Nose, Extraordinary discharge from	Monk's Hood
Obesity, Bodily infirmity through	Mares-Tail
Paralysed Limbs, Tincture for	Heather (Medicinal Virtues)
Perspiration, Colds and Chills after	Monk's Hood
Poison which causes Gout and Rheumatism	Mountain Ash
Premature Ageing	Coral
Prostration on least exertion	Pæony
Prostration, Sense of	Elm Tree
Pulse	Fir Tree
Recovery: specific remedy for depletion and want of vigour after long illness	Lime Tree
Recovery: specific remedy for depletion and want of vigour after long illness	Wood-Sorrel
Restlessness	Brook-Lime, Monk's Hood, St John's Wort
Rheumatism	Mountain Ash
Scarlatina, Poison in the Blood after	Lichen
Scrofula, Germinal	Clematis
Senses, Quickener of	Coral
Skin Diseases and skin eruptions of all kinds	Poppy
Skin Diseases, Scaly	Lichen
Sleeplessness	Brook-Lime, Poppy, Crimson Corn

Sluggish Nature	Gold
Sneezing	Monk's Hood
Spinal Affections	Holly Tree
Spinal Cord	Brook-Lime
Spinal Irritation	Brook-Lime
Spleen, Generation of Life Forces through the	Pæony
Stomach	Poplar Tree
Stupor (Narcotic like state)	Poppy, Crimson Corn
Suffocation, Sense of	Box Tree
Thighs, Intense pain in	Clematis
Throat, Great Heat in the	Holly Tree
Timidity	Oak Tree
Tiredness after sleep	Poppy, Crimson Corn
Toothache	Crane's Bill
Tumours	Alder Tree, Wood-Sorrel, Ash Tree
Ulcers	Alder Tree
Uric Acid	Mountain Ash
Vitality	Crane's Bill, Wood-Sorrel
Vitality: Physically Strengthens and Vivifies the Vital and Generative Forces	Carbuncle
Weakness — an all gone feeling	Oak Tree
Weakness, affecting the Chest	Ferns
Weakness: A sinking without pain.	Pæony
Weakness: A giver of Strength and Vigour	Lime Tree

Soul, A Strengthener and Fortifier against evil and wicked persons   Topaz

Soul, A Strengthener, Healer, and Comforter of the   St John's Wort

Soul, Disburdener of the Oppressed   Ruby

Soul: A connector to   Turquoise

Soul: Discord on the Soul plane   Orange Tribe

Soul: Morbid Effluvia, which, like a horrid nightmare,
clings to the helpless Soul   Yew Tree

Wisdom   Emerald

Orders for Old and Modern Works on Occult Philosophy and Kindred Subjects may be sent to the Editor.

The following rare and valuable works can be had in manuscript form or typed.

1. A perfect and original copy of the *Keys of Rabbi Solomon*. Translated from the Hebrew into English, the whole embellished by a vast number of mysterious Figures, Talismans, Pentacles, Quandaries, Circles, and Characters.

    Copies of this can be made at £7 7s. 0d. each.

2. *Culpeper's Last Legacies*. Febrilia, or a Treatise of Fevers in general, by Nicholas Culpeper, 1656.

    Composita or a Synopsis of the Chiefest Compositions in use now with Galenists, 1656.

    Medicine here very well arranged to the various Diseases with properties, etc.

    A Treatise on the Pestilence with Prevision, Provision, and Prevention, etc., for 1656.

    Aphorisms, etc. Exceedingly useful for all Diseases to the various Organs of the Body with all the Ancient Receipts, Syrups, Oils, Tinctures, Waters, Wines, Pills. etc.

    Copies of this can be made at £7 7s. 0d. each.

From the Editor:–

MR R. WELCH, TYLDESLEY, NR. MANCHESTER, ENGLAND.

PSYCHOLOGY OF BOTANY

A TREATISE ON

TREES, SHRUBS, AND PLANTS, ETC.,

FOR THE

CURE OF DISEASES AND AILMENTS,

OF THE

HUMAN SYSTEM, (WITHOUT MEDICINE),

By

SYMPATHY (POSITIVE AND NEGATIVE:) ON THE SOUL PLANE, BY

"CHARUBEL" (THE GREAT SEER).

A Collegian who trained for the Gospel 60 years ago, gave his
whole life up for the love of Nature and the Study of
the Supernatural Elements, &c., &c.

Author of The Zodiac Symbolized, The Psychic Mirror, The
North Pole Star and Region, The Seer Critic,
The Geozonic Spheres, The Occultist, Astrographical
Revelations, Psychological Experiences, &c.

---

*"But yet these truths being never so certain, never so clear, he may be
Ignorant of either, or all of them, who will never take the pains to employ
his faculties as he should to inform himself about them."*

John Locke.

Leigh :
Percy R. Paine, Printer, 5, Union Street,
Published by R. Welch, Esq., 92, Shuttle Street, Tyldesley,
1906.